maybe someday,

MAYBE SOMEDAY

914

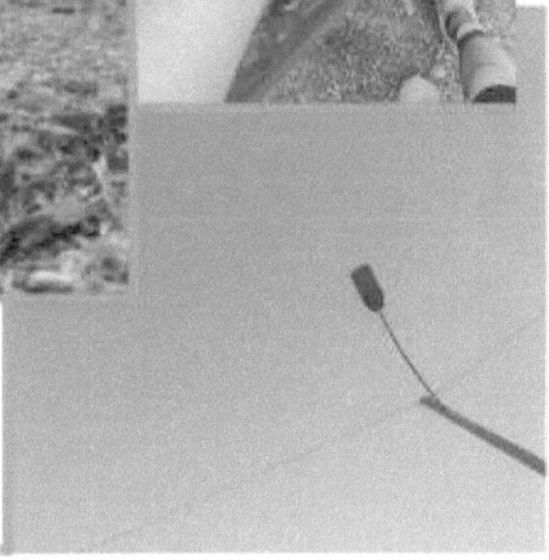

^ . < _

by Jaedon Blocker

(a.k.a. Arranging the

While every precaution has been taken in the preparation of this book, the publisher assumes no responsibility for errors or omissions, or for damages resulting from the use of the information contained herein.

MAYBE SOMEDAY, MAYBE SOMEDAY

First edition. April 10, 2024.

Dedication

If you've been a part of this journey,

you know who you are,

and I appreciate you :)

You are all a piece of me,

no matter how big or small that piece is

You have shaped who I am,

and your fingerprints will always be there

on the surface of my life

Though I wrote all of these poems by myself

and for myself,

I could never have made it through this process,

or ever even begun to try publishing them,

Without you,

so...

Thank you!

And thank *you*, reader,

for being interested in my story and supporting my passion

That truly means so much to me!

Arranging the Pieces

Let your heart be open,
　even if no one receives it
Say what you mean,
　even if no one believes it
Live your life,
　like you don't need a reason
Because we're all broken,
　and we're just arranging the pieces.

Preface

I started writing this book on the day I almost killed myself: July 21, 2020. However, I didn't know it yet at the time. It was about 10:45pm, and I was in my bed, crying, wrapping the sheets around my head and neck, listening to Odyssey by Talos, trying to cut off my airflow and suffocate myself to death. That was plan A, and if that didn't work, plan B was to run out into the interstate just down the street. Seventeen years old. "Unloosen the sky / And suffer the sights / Then you walked out in raging water." As my sheets became flooded with my tears, my breath became harder to find. I felt my head getting numb and my consciousness looking for an escape. "Our temples are hearts / And then heaven alee / Heavy the final force / And I was downed in dying water." All of a sudden, a flash of red forcefully illuminated my mind, and I thought maybe this is it; this is the door to my death, but instead, I sensed my arms frantically pulling at the sheets around my head, tangling through the knots, until I saw the faint light in my bedroom and desperately reached for my phone, which laid on the floor beside my bed, though not quite knowing why I needed it like my life depended on it. "I wake to your likeness / But how come you're here? / I wasn't found in delight / *It's the call before it's far from over.*" I paused Odyssey and opened my Google Docs app, and before I knew it, I had written something. Something I called Arrange. It's a weird feeling, the feeling of being alive when you thought you wouldn't be. The tears kept falling. I was still more depressed than ever. I still hated myself. I still wanted my life to be over. But I was alive. "Now I'm wading water / Then I'm cast out in the cold / Heave that light up over you / . . . / Fading right, *just once,* you know." Looking back, I now realize that red flash was not the door to my death; it was the door to hope. And in that moment, I took my first step toward it. The next morning I woke up with a new sense of light. A speck of stardust in a universe of darkness but a light nonetheless. And from that day on, I wrote. These words became my therapist, my coping mechanism, my escape, my best friend, my hope. This was the beginning of *Maybe Someday, Maybe Someday*. I spent the next year and a half writing words (I didn't even realize it was poetry until I had written just about everything in this book). I wrote these purely just to help myself make it through each day without any intention of ever sharing them, let alone publishing them, but here I am. Seventeen and eighteen were two of my darkest years, so most of the poems in here are not pretty, elegant, and happy; they are the truth, my truth. But that doesn't mean they are without hope or without a positive message because I found some sense of hope through these words and want to make a positive impact on others with them. We are all broken, and we're just arranging the pieces. Writing this poetry was my attempt to begin arranging *my* brokenness. Each poem in this collection is a piece of me, and I hope that as you read it, you may find pieces of yourself in my words and come out of it feeling more complete than before. And maybe someday, maybe someday...*you will realize* you were whole all along.

"In this odyssey / It's hard to leave / I hold at the breach /
I've got my reasons."

Table of Contents

Chapter 3: EIGHTEEN, pt. II

Chapter 1:
SEVENTEEN

July 21, 2020 — December 31, 2020

^ • < –

Arrange

Lost
Lost
Lost
What else of me?
Lost
What me of else?
Lost

Stay? Or move on?
Change? Or remain?

Stay. Move on.
Change. Remain. Rearrange.

So much yet so little
So strong yet so brittle
So complex yet so simple
Why, in this world of waves, do I continue to feel like no more than a
ripple?

Lost

Stay? Or move on?
Change? Or remain?

Stay. Move on.
Change. Remain. Rearrange.

Stay. Move on.
Change and rearrange.

Found?...
Lost

To be so much, but how to do it?
When I'm the only one to get me through it?
No one to help
No one to guide
But is that really the truth that I believe in?
Have I come this far just to leave then?
No, but I can't, still I have to go on
Can't lose my faith in what's only begun
How can I help?
How can I guide?

Stay. Move on.
Change. Remain. Rearrange.

Stay. Move on.
Change. Arrange.

All of these pieces lay around me
But when will I be able to arrange all of this hopeful brokenness
And live a better life?

Live Less

Everything I do just makes me hate myself more
Every moment I live just makes me want to live less
Everyone I meet makes me question what I'm living for
Everything I do seems to fail though I always try my best
And I keep on trying and I'm always so obsessed
With all the ways I want to live but still I want to live less

Every way that I look at it, my life is broken in design
Everywhere I go leads down a path of no success
Everyone seems to think that I'm doing just fine
And I won't tell them I'm not to keep that weight off their chests
And I keep on crying because it's my only defense
Against all these thoughts that make me want to live less

You gave me the tool, but I couldn't use it
Everything I do, further proves that I'm useless
You say I'm wrong, well, why don't you prove it?
I tried to make things better, but I know that I blew it
And I could try again, but you know that won't do it
Because my doubts and depression have all grown so ruthless
I have tried to find the answers but I'm still so clueless
And without the sun, my night sky is moonless

Every cell in my body is so full of doubt
Every night I think back it just makes me depressed
Every time I get lost I just look for ways out
I don't want to die but still I want to live less
I'm sure that to you, this doesn't make sense

It's like life is my enemy, but the only friend I possess

I know that the answers are out there to find
Maybe someday I'll make a home of this mess
For year after year, I've been at war with my mind
And I've thought of just laying my weapons to rest
But I want every moment I live to make me want to live more
And everything I do to make me hate myself less

How can I learn to not want to live less?

Scarred (by the Scarred)

Scarred by the scarred; scar the unscarred
Wonder how far, this hate of ours
Can burn in our hearts, until it's all gone too far
How could I come this far, for it to all fall apart?

So many questions; questioning my questions
So many important things that nobody mentions
So many terrible actions made with innocent intentions
So many answers that don't answer our questions

Scarred by the scarred; scar the unscarred
Wonder how far, this hate of ours
Can burn in our scars, until it all falls apart
And then where can we start?

Scarred by the scarred; scar the unscarred
Wonder how far, this hate of ours
Can burn in our scars, until it all falls apart
And we can make a new start

Fall

So quick to destroy without a second thought
So eager to crumble the beauty we've got
Always willing to cause harm to it all
Just to make another fall

Keep on going, don't look back
Never stop, stop to think
About the waste, you create
Keep on going, don't look back
Never stop, stop to think
About the ways, you could create

Take a moment, take a breath
Always stop, stop to think
About the waste, we create
Take a moment, take a breath
Always stop, stop to think
About the ways, we could create

Why are we so quick to destroy without a second thought?
And so eager to crumble the beauty we've got
Always willing to cause harm to it all
Just to make another fall
Why are we so quick to hate without a second thought?
So eager to ruin the love that we've got
Always willing to cause harm to us all
Just to make another fall

The innocent corrosion and destructive intentions
The intense emotion and pent up tensions
We live an explosion and build up possessions
All losing hope in the chance it would lessen
This path that we've chosen is a sure-to-be dead end
I don't care about you if you're not my best friend
Selfish actions won't lead us to heaven
Maybe someday we will all learn our lesson

Too

I am feeling lost right now
Where to go, what to do
How to make it up to you
When I don't even know where I am right now
They say keep moving on
So I'll keep moving on
But I'll keep looking back
Though I know that it's wrong
And I'll try to remake
What I've made of my life
In the hopes that you will
Too

To Be Me

Everybody tells me to just be myself
It's okay to be different and have some flaws
That's what makes you who you are
But every time I do, people just complain and say that it's wrong
I'm being difficult and not doing the right things
So what am I supposed to do?
When no matter what I do, I'm always wrong
I just want to be a good person
But don't want to pretend to be someone else in order to be seen as one
I'm just trying my best to be me
But is that wrong?
Is it wrong for me to want to just be me?
Is that wrong?

People tell me that I should accept myself for who I am
And never judge another for who they are
But those are the same people who judge me most and try to change me
I try my best to please the people around me
But I can't get myself to be someone who I'm not
I'm just trying my best to be me
But is that wrong?
Is it wrong for me to want to just be me?
Is that wrong?

Am I really that bad?
Can someone trying so hard to be perfect truly be the worst of all?
I hate myself, and I hate what I do
But I would never want to be anyone else

I truly like the way I think and the things that I believe
But I still hate myself, and still hate what I do
I don't expect myself to be flawless or for everyone to like me
But I don't understand how I can try so hard to do my best
And still just feel so wrong
I feel so wrong
Is it wrong for me to feel this way?
Is it wrong?
Is that wrong?

I'm just trying my best to be me
But is that wrong?
Is it wrong for me to want to just be me?
Is that wrong?

Bad to be Good

I want to protect the world from all the bad
Make it better and preserve its life
Stop all the evil from destroying the beauty
Rid this earth of all the terrible people
But though it's for good, does this make me bad?

Then people will want to protect the world from me
Make it better by destroying my life
Stop all my evil from destroying the beauty
Rid this earth of all my terrible evil
But though it's for good, does this make us bad?

It's just so sad and it hurts so much
It makes me mad, but it just seems like

You have to kill to save lives
Have to be bad to be good
We have to blow things up to make it safe
Is it bad to be good?
It can't be right that you should
Have to be bad to be good
Is it bad to be good?

If you were to kill a man who had killed
If you were to hate a man for being hateful
If you were to wrong a man who was wrong
If you were to destroy a man because he destroyed
Even though you want to do it for good

Would that be wrong?

I know it's sad and it hurts so much
We've all gone mad, but it just seems like

You have to kill to save lives
Have to be bad to be good
We have to blow things up to make it safe
Is it bad to be good?
It can't be right that you should
Have to be bad to be good
Is it bad to be good?

There must be another way
A way to be good
Without being bad
It can't be bad
Bad to be good

If you
Were to
Kill
Me
Because of all the bad things that I've done
Would that...
Would that...
Be wrong?

This Is All I Can Be

I was walking along down the street with my friends
When we wandered into a forest around one of the bends
Not thinking much, just trying to escape
From the stress of the lives that we live every day
Relaxing our minds and having some fun
Not caring what's happening or what could go wrong
How could we live in that previous state?
We can never go back to living that way

But as we trudge onward, I begin to see
Dark, little, creeping imperfections all around me
The twigs twisting and turning to get in my way
The clouds crawling in quickly to block out the day
The flow of the flowers falls out of synchronization
And even the ants are all growing impatient
I barely even notice as my friends fade away
Because, in the cusp of this calamity, this is all I can be

I try to move forward, feeling numb and alone
But my vision is blurry, and my feet are asleep
Pound them into the ground, and rub my eyes a few times
I try to get going but then realize
There's a big figure hiding out in the brush
I hear it draw nearer, sounding ferocious and gruff
Frozen in place, I see its big angry face
I break out of my daze and, acting with celerity, I decide to run

But where do I go? I know I cannot stay here
I must flee from all this great danger and fear
But it feels like my feet are magnetized to the ground
I've got to keep running or soon I'll be found
I'm swimming through mud and I'm falling through sand
I wish my friends were here, but would they understand?
Could they help? Would they help?
Would they be too scared?
I think it's better they're safe

More and more beasts coming out of the trees
It's obviously clear that they're following me
They smell the sweet taste of a victim who's already lost
How can I keep going when I've already lost?
That's when the swarm came flooding in
Swooping in from every angle and piercing my skin
Finding their way in deeper and blinding my view
I try to stop them, but there's nothing I can do

All these dark, little bats around me fluttering
Cluttering my thoughts, I can't think straight
All I hear are the words that they're quietly uttering
Thisisallyoucanbethisisallyoucanbethisisallyoucanbethisisallyoucanbe

THISISALLYOUCANBETHISISALLYOUCANBE, I yell in agreement
with my new army
I feel so strong and so fearless, screaming together in harmony, I feel free
The beasts come charging full-force; bring them on, let the come
For they are not ready for what I'm about to become
There's nothing I can't be!

There's nothing I can't be!

Just then, one of the beasts bursts through the great curtain of darkness
It breaks down the walls protecting my vulnerability
As if at my peak, I was at my greatest weakness
Like my great increase in power was the source of my increased frailty

As he approaches, he stares me straight in the eyes
I stare sternly back, ready to meet my demise
And we slowly sink deeper; I think I see something lighter inside
But wait–

I shoot up and I scream
I look around frantically and see
All the darkness is gone, was it all a dream?
Oh, but how can it be? I saw it all so clearly

Were the bats ever there?
Or did they just go away?
Were the beasts of my nightmares
Really there to destroy me?
Did I let this all happen?
Could I have avoided it all?
Is this really what I was meant to be?
This is not what I want to be, but...

This is all I can be?
Is this all I can be?

This is all I can be

This is all I can be!
How can this be!?
Oh, how can this be!!?

–

So remember, when everything seems to be going all wrong all around you
Don't make it worse than it needs to be
You don't have to embrace it, but don't let it destroy you
It will make you into something you don't want to be

Because,
When reality becomes the worst possibility, there is no other way it can
possibly be
This is all you can be
Even when truly it's not what you see, your worrying mind just cannot
agree
You see, you just need to believe, that things may be better than how they
may seem
And how you perceive, is something no one else sees, something only you
can be
So please, try not to deceive, yourself and relieve, all the burdens and
thoughts that you always carry
Because they're all you can be
Unless you don't let them be

Kitty

On the way to get the water
For my parents' morning coffee
I was caught by surprise by a little figure
Laying there under the water dispenser

Did he see me, could he feel me?
As I shuffled past, not realizing
That this little moment would change who I am and how I exist
And bring such great meaning
To my life and hopefully yours

It just goes to show...
The time you share...
Make the most...
Make the most of every moment...
Take care...
Take care,
Kitty

I look closer, it's shivering
A little mouse on the floor
How did he get here?
Is he alive?
Please, be alive

What do I do?
Can I help? How can I help?
Is it too late?

deep breath
"Umm, hey, I think there's like a little mouse or something under the
water dispenser thing," I yell out to my brother
He picks him up and wraps him in a cloth
Makes sure he's warm and safe and has something to eat
Why can't I do this? He does it with such ease
Helps him be comfortable and have whatever he needs
I wish I could have done more, but I love you, our little Kitty

No one knew how long you would last
But we all felt like you'd be here forever
Made you a home in an old Valentines box
And you seemed so content lying under the blanket
Here in our house, up on the shelf in the corner
And you could have been wherever with anyone
But you were here with us, in your final moments

It just goes to show that your time may short
And the time you share with those you were meant to be with may not
last
To make the most of every moment and take care of each other
Is all we can do to make our time count
I hope I made your time count, Kitty

Did you know you were going?
Oh, Kitty—Oh, Kitty
How were you feeling?
Oh, Kitty—Oh, Kitty
Did we do what was right?
Oh, Kitty—Oh, Kitty

To make your last few hours feel alright?
Oh, Kitty
Oh, Kitty
Could we have made your time longer?
Or would you have died right there under the water dispenser
Had I not seen you there and called my brother over?
Were you just trying to get your last drink of water
On that cold evening in October?
Oh, Kitty
Oh, Kitty
I hope I made your time count
I'm sorry if I didn't make your time count

Now your body lays there in the old Valentines box
And I can't believe that it took until now
For me to have the courage to touch your fur
To make that connection between me and you
And I know how short our time can be
So I promise this moment will be something I remember
And I will make more of the time I have with others in the future
I love you, Kitty, my little mousey friend, I'll remember forever

I hope I made your time count
Your short, short time
We made it count
You made my time count, you made our time count,
Kitty

Confined

I feel confined
With all these thoughts coming to life in my mind
The ideas I've designed but not yet refined
My dreams and desires that are all kept inside
Trying to burst out from this cage that they're all trapped behind
I want to let them all out and enjoy the ride
Let these seeds bear their fruits and find the secrets they hide
I can't bear to see them just rot and I've tried
To bring these thoughts to fruition but I just can't find
Ways to express this expression in successful succession and get myself out
of this state of depression, live the life I envision that I probably could if I
just made the decision, but I can't, and I can't, and I can't, and I can't, and
I can't stand to just sit here and let the walls grow thicker
Will they fall if I wait?
Why won't they come down quicker?
Can I say all that I want without feeling confined?
I want to say all that I need without feeling confined

But I still feel confined

I feel confined
And I still can't find
A way to unwind
And clear out my mind
My ideas and doubts have become so intertwined
It's getting harder to tell what is wrong and what's right
I want to make art and write poems and make beautiful places to visit
I want to say things and for people to listen

I want to be a painter, a poet; an architect of the future
I want to make things and not be the only viewer

But I still feel confined

Maybe someday I'll find
A way to not feel confined

unfinishing Touches

I look at all these things I've written
All these things that I have done
And I keep thinking to myself
Are they ever really done?
What makes these things complete?
Is there more I could have done?
Can I make all these things better if I just give a bit more?
So I keep on adding these unfinishing touches
But they'll never be complete
They will never be complete

I think about this poem
And all the ways it could be different
The endless possibilities
And all the ways it could be better
Just a simple thought turned into something bigger
But just because it's big doesn't mean that it can't grow
Can I take my thoughts a little farther?
Will it be complete with one more verse?
Should I keep on adding on more details?
Or will that just make it worse?
I keep on adding these unfinishing touches
But it'll never be complete
It will never be complete

For many years I've lived
And many years I will live more
But there's so much I haven't done

And so much that I don't know
Can I break from the confines that exist in my life?
Can I live the life I want?
Can I ever reach all of my goals?
Or will I then just want much more?
Should I try to live the way I am?
Or is it better if I change?
I want to truly see myself, but I lack so many pieces
Pieces I must find, pieces I must arrange
But will I ever understand it all, understand it all before…
…before—
I keep on adding these unfinishing touches
But I'll never be complete
I will never be complete

I will never
I will never
I will never

I will never…

Toulouse

Toulouse
Toulouse
To lose
To lose
Toulouse, Toulose
To lose Toulouse

You had Toulouse
You had to lose
You had Toulouse
You had to lose

And you yearn Toulouse
You'll learn to lose
Still you yearn Toulouse
But you learned to lose

Would you keep him here if you could choose?
Or was it right for him to be set loose?
Does his absence leave a swelling bruise?
Or does it settle your heart? I guess you choose

Oh, but you had to lose
You had to lose

You had to lose
Toulouse
Toulouse

You had to lose
Toulouse
Toulouse

You mourn Toulouse
You do
You do
You forswore Toulouse?
Did you?
Did you?

Do you allow his absence
To swallow
You
Or do you frame up the views?
You choose
You choose

You choose to lose
Who knew, Toulouse?
But you don't accuse
We love you, Toulouse

Though you chose to lose
Heaven knows the truth
Toulouse, Toulouse
Heaven holds Toulouse

Lost Words - Interlude

Two of the poems that were supposed to be a part of this chapter, Tomato Garden and Cross-eyed, I was not able to include because they have been lost. I remember I wrote both of these while I was in class on some random paper I had available, but unfortunately they went missing before I was able to 'eternalize' them into my phone. Both of these poems were *incredibly* special to me, so it greatly pains me to know I will more than likely never get to read them in their true, original form ever again. Maybe someday I will be sorting through some old stuff and they will present themselves to me again, but I won't get my hopes up about it because it probably won't happen. However, I would like to ask *you* a favor. I remember the concept behind both of these poems, so I would like to share that with you and let you write your own version of them. And maybe *your words* can make up for my lost words.

Tomato Garden was a poem I wrote for my grandmother who died when I was 6. She was really special to me and I remember just shortly before she died, she invited me to start a tomato garden with her in her backyard, and I was *so* excited about it. However, unfortunately we didn't get too far before she died of a stroke in April. With my writing, I tried to make a comparison between the incompleteness of the tomato garden we were excited to grow and the incompleteness of our lives at death with all the things we still dream of doing that are left unreached. Things that are left unsettled. I wondered if she felt like her life was incomplete or if she was satisfied with how far she had grown, even if she never got to bear her full fruits and reap all the rewards of her hard work throughout her life.

Cross-eyed was a poem I specifically remember was written in my senior-year AP Lit. class just shortly after we were able to return to in-person classes during the COVID pandemic. We were required to have these big, clear guards on our desks that somewhat isolated us from the other students. The borders along each edge of it were really distracting for my eyes, and, as I tried to focus on the lesson on the board, my eyes kept getting stuck, almost cross-eyed, on these fabric borders right in front of my face. I related this experience with how I tend to get really in my head about everything to an extremely overwhelming level. An unhealthy level. So I thought of how I am always looking inward in comparison to crossing your eyes. When you cross your eyes, you can't see very well, and if you do it long enough—at least I've been told—they can get stuck like that. So if I keep looking into my own head so much, I won't be able to truly see and navigate my life very well and may end up getting stuck in my head, trapped there forever. So this poem was me working through all that, and, in the end, trying to get myself to start widening my vision to break away from my own mind and see the world in front of me clearly for once.

I would love for you to use the space provided for each to write your own version of Tomato Garden and Cross-eyed. Of course, you can write absolutely whatever you want. The page is yours. You don't have to write anything like what I've described if you don't want to, but I've left that there for you if you want to take my idea and place it like a garden in the backyard of your mind, plant your thoughts and feelings into its dirt, and grow your own words from the soil of my idea.

And maybe *together* we can finish that tomato garden and learn to escape from the cage of our cross-eyed minds.

P.S. – I would love for you to share your writing with me
on Instagram @arranging_the_pieces if you want to

Tomato Garden

Cross-eyed

Chapter 2:
EIGHTEEN, pt. I

January 1, 2021 — July 21, 2021

^ • < —

Focus On The Moon

Out in the night
Barely a cloud in the sky
But you can't see the ground
In the endless darkness surrounding you
Just focus on the moon
Focus on the moon
Focus on the moon

The trees blur the boundary between above and below
You can't find your way out, can't find your way home
The sea searches, growing rougher as it flows
It can drown your heart out, as its beat starts to slow
The leaves rustle loudly, breathing all you've ever known
You lose sight of what's ahead, you lose sight of home
But although you feel like you may have lost all of your hope
Just focus on the moon, it'll lead you home

Just focus on the moon
Focus on the moon
Focus on the moon
Let the stars fill your view
They'll take care of you
You'll be safe soon
Just focus on the moon

The serpent of your sorrow binds you up inside its coils
Its constriction holds you tight
You'll slowly suffocate here, but you know, but you know

An infection from its bite
As you walk on through the forest, every step becomes a struggle
No protection from the plight
Let yourself be illuminated by the moon's glow, by the moon's glow
A reflection of the light

Take the bit of light you have and find your way
Fix your eyes, try to focus, clear your head of the pain
And as the mud piles on your clothes, colors covered by cracked clay
No matter what, — don't be deceived, it's not a stain

Just focus on the moon
Focus on the moon
Focus on the moon
Let the stars fill your view
They'll take care of you
You'll be safe soon
Just focus on the moon

Pull it in a little closer
And let it lift up the tide
So the water can wash away your pain

Just focus on the moon
Focus on the moon
Focus on the moon
With all that life has put you through
Looking on the bright side's not an easy thing to do
So just hold on, hold the hope you have
The sun will come out soon

Just focus on the moon

Focus on the moon

Focus on the moon

Focus on the moon

Seafloor

Hidden in a sphere of glass
I found an ocean
An ocean full of water, deep and blue
Standing in a field of grass
I feel the morning dew that coats its edges after last night's rain
And I'm no longer satisfied with the dew

I dip my toes in, test the water
Gradually release, little by little
A rougher current, it's touch grows colder
Try to retract, but she appears and pulls me in
And I'm not fighting, pull me under
This is what I've chosen, I chose her
This is what I've chosen, take me farther
Take me farther, deeper water
Take me farther, to the seafloor

I found a lover on the seafloor
We slept together in the seabed
We made love until we reached the shore
But then the tide pulled us back in

I can't feel the waves down here
I don't feel the pressure from above
Though the weight of the ocean holds me down
It's the way it holds me tight that I have grown to love

And my air tank's running out
But I don't care
Because I found some comfort in the depths of your blue
I'll set my anchor in the rubble
I'll drown here with you

I found a lover on the seafloor
We slept together in the seabed
We made love until we reached the shore
But then the tide pulled us back in

I'll drown here with you
I'll drown here with you
Let the tide pull me in
You'll drown here with me
My lover in the sea
You'll drown here with me

The scales in the sky point the way for me to go
I don't think I should be here; I think it's time for me to go

I'll drown you out of me!
I'll drown you out of me!
The tide can't pull me back in!
You'll drown without me!
My lover of the sea!
You'll drown here, you'll see...

I found a lover on the seafloor
We slept together in the seabed

We made love until we reached the shore
But then the tide pulled her back in

I'll be satisfied with the dew

Walk Out The Door Together

When your colors came together
You created a connection
With the purple of your eyes
And his that are so green
Your colors became brighter
And you gave each other your protection
Bringing vibrancy to your skies
And feeling safer than you've ever been
You have such different pasts but want the same future
Even with the differences you've seen
He loves your purple
And you love his green

Walk through the door together
Take off your shoes and hang your coats
Wearing your new matching sweaters
Walk into the warmth of home

As your time together ages
Your bond becomes a tether
The chambers of your hearts have been constricted
Your eyes can't handle all this weather
Through the wind and rain that you've endured
Your colors start to fade
Your purple now a dull lilac
And his green a lightened jade
There's nothing left that you can say
And now you will...

Walk out the door together
Put on your shoes and grab your coats
Wear them over matching sweaters
Walk out into the cold alone

You walk out into the cold alone
Walk out into the cold alone
But don't forget the love you've shown
Even though you're now alone
Walk out into the cold alone
Walk out into the cold alone
And though, this love, you have outgrown
Just know you're not alone

Find yourself a shade of yellow
And he will find his red

HOME, forever

The grass has all turned brown
But I wish that it was green
Chlorophyll come fill this space
And bring life back to this scene
I want to finish off this season in the comfort of my home
But have a field of life to go to when I don't wanna be alone
If you make me leave here now, with this tainted view in mind
I will never get these memories back, no matter how much I rewind
And I won't remember this time as being right all the way up to the end
But we're so close, so can't we please just stay even if it's just pretend
'Cause I can't bear to leave this lawn alone
I'll miss this pond that's my oasis
This view from the bay window, so attached to I have grown
Pulls me right out of my head when I'm in a place of stasis
And the blue from my room, holding a home of life within its three
brown frames
And I'm oh-so alone, holding this home of mine within my own frail
brain

I know they say the grass is greener on the other side
But the grass was always green here 'til that February night
When my parents had an argument that turned into a fight
And I just sat there silent, crying, knowing neither one was right
And I don't care if it's greener
This is my home and I prefer
To stay here for the future
But you say one day I'll learn
To love the new place

And I say "whatever"
There's no way to measure
The great amount of pressure
That you've put me under
But for now, I'll just gather
All the strength I can muster
I know for you two it must hurt
To lose a once-lover
But I still remain flustered
So scared of what may come after
It's all become just a vague blur
Could you do me a favor?
And save this for later
When I'm out of this house
You can go live wherever
When I'm out of your life
The two of you can sever
I'm not one to lash out
And let loose all my anger
Except in the words on this paper
I AM THE ARRANGER
In my story, I'm the writer
Inside myself, an outsider
All my pieces are scattered
And continue to shatter
This is not what I'm after
But what does it matter?
I sense the incoming closure
Soon our life will be over
One day, we'll all become strangers

Cold and drifting, like glaciers
I've made my mind, but can't change hers
Still I try to persuade her
You say it over and over
"You can do it different when it's your turn"
And I will, I'll do better
I'll make my home HOME forever

. . . .

I'm the only one left
But are you the survivors?
I'll wait here as it goes up in fire
My happily ever after
While you sit there in comfort
I hear the faint sound of laughter
And for a moment I'd rather
Be there with you all together
And I'll be happier after
Maybe, but I can't; let me stay here
Let's stay here forever

Equator

You found me
When you were stretched across your globe
And I bound you
In all the comfort that I know
Words sounding
From those around you thought you loved
And they send you
To your farthest below and above

At your coldest, driest points
Separated from yourself with a whole world in between
Your melting will soon be settled
As I step into the scene

If you're the poles
Then I'm the equator
Bridge the gap along the prime meridian
And bring you back into your center

I fell in deep
So scared of what you thought
I lay so low
Trapped by the doubts and worried that I brought
And I can't sleep
Because the thought of losing has me fraught
But I don't know
Whether it's all even real or not

At my coldest, driest points
Separated from myself with a whole world in between
My melting will soon be settled
As you step into the scene

If I'm the poles
Then you're the equator
Bridge the gap along the prime meridian
And bring me back out to my center

When you're the poles
I'll be your equator
With all they stole
I'll be the mediator
When I'm the poles
You'll be my equator
You'll be my equator
I'll be your equator

If we're both the poles
We'll be each other's equator
Though we may each have such different caves we're in
We'll pull each other back to our center
We'll bring ourselves back to the equator

And there we'll be together
Until you get lost again and start to wander
Back out to the places that make you suffer
But just know that you matter
I'll bring you back to the equator

Everything You Do

You say that you struggle to express all your true feelings
You say I'm pretty swag but I know what that truly means
It's fine, you take your time, I'll be ready when your heart's ready to sing
And I'll listen, I'll let it sink in, and then join in to complete the harmony
It's the least I can do when you've done so much for me
It's the right thing to do when you mean so much to me

Thanks so much for everything you do!
Thank you for being you!

I know I should be doing more
I want to give you all I can, yes you
But believe me that I'll try
I know I can do better
I want to be the best I can, for you
But it might take me some time

When I'm upset with you
When you make me angry
When I start doubting you
When my thoughts betray me
Please remember, it's not your fault and I don't hate you
Though that's how it may seem
You're someone, you are someone who
I'm not okay with losing

Thanks so much for everything you do!
Thanks! I want to make it up to you

Thank you! I'll do whatever I can do
To make a happy you

I'd do anything to make you smile
It would make it all worth my while
And even when our flaws begin to show
I really just want you to know
I appreciate everything you do
I truly appreciate you

Thank you, for being you!

Around The Lake /// Sticks

Blooming, like the tulips that surround us
We walk the circles of those around us
I want to go outward and see where it can take us
You hesitantly follow, seeing only dead ends, but they can't save us

Across the bridge, we walk through a place of reconstruction
The parts we don't understand yet, a barren landscape that's recovering
Slide through the dividers, we take a risk but slide back out before we're questioned
Couldn't quite get our hole-in-one but still we keep on walking

As we make our way around the lake
We make our way around the lake
Can't lose sight, because the journey's what we make
This is what we make, as we make our way around the lake

More than seven
But not quite twenty
It's always the hard parts
I'm always overestimating

Is this too far?
Should we have not come out this way?
Can't turn back now
Finish it out now before I regret yesterday

Banished from its waters
But it's still there
It's still there inside you
And still in me

Brought together, the 10th of 4
Thought we wouldn't make it
But we pulled it back in time before
The 11 showed their faces

We'll both see the ledge next time we're at the lake
I'm so sorry that it couldn't be today
But I'm so glad we made this journey and I still said it on that date
I just want to do what's right, but you know I couldn't wait

///

You break me, like twigs in your hands
But I grow back stronger than before
And I'm beginning to understand
That this is why I love you more and more
Someday, I'll bring you a bouquet of branches
Strong and sturdy, full of life
One day, I'll have the courage to ask you
Hey, would you please be my—
No, not yet
I'm not ready
But maybe someday
Maybe someday

We still have more sticks to break

Eight

A pure and hopeful soul
Tainted by the truth
Won't take in a word you're told
Don't believe their lies
They chip away at my fragile mold
Punctured by their words
Latch on tightly to the life I hold
Don't let in the curse

And the world lost a little more light
That night
And the world gained a little more pain
That day
In my mind, starts a brittle new fight
That night
And my heart gained a little more weight
That day

You were eight
And I was fourteen
But I'm still eight
While you keep growing
So why is it that you can be so fine
When you had it so much worse than me?
While I'm still stuck here in my mind
Holding onto things I can't unsee

And my soul reaped the fruits of my mind

It's not right
And I won't let it hurt is what I say
Though it may
And it's still blocking out all my sight
I can't fight
Will I live to see another day?
I can't stay

All my hate
And it's still growing
All this hate
I gained from knowing
I try, great
But it keeps showing
All this hate
I hate my knowing

How can I live with all this truth in my life?
How can I live with all the truth in their lies?
How do you live with all that truth in your life?
How can I keep going and how can I thrive?

Then the world will gain a little more light
Sometime
Then the world will lose a little more pain
Someday
In my mind, will end a war with a truce I write
Stops the fight
And my heart will let down a little more weight
It would be great

But for now, I hold onto these feelings
And all the parts of me that they're stealing
But for now, I'll try to keep listening
To all the advice that you're bringing
And maybe someday, maybe someday, I can start compromising
There's no way to change their minds, I'm now realizing
It's not easy, but please just know that I'm trying
To accept all these facts and still keep the eight-year-old in me thriving

I'll keep the eight-year-old in me thriving
Please keep the eight-year-old in you thriving
I'll keep him from dying
Please keep her from dying

But we still keep on growing
We'll keep growing with our knowing
Knowing that the truth is never slowing
We'll keep on growing with our knowing

Archipelago

We're a cluster of islands
In a big body of life
In the center you and I stand
From the depths of the sea
Up to the sunlight
Surrounded by all of our family and friends
It all feels just right
As connections are made, the earth's crust, it bends
Change the view over night
But if I have to stray as my currents command
I'm worried that you will not stay
But they say love never ends
So I guess it will all be okay

I trust things will be fine when I leave this archipelago
But still, I just can't let go
'Cause while I'm gone, I will never know
How the islands reshape, until I get home

As my tectonic plates start to shift
I know I'll return
In reality it won't be too long
But I know
I know well a lot can happen in that time
New islands will emerge
Some sink down in the sea
Some may collide and come together
Forming new, bigger land

Others may shift and separate over time
But will my island still fit in right where it did before?

I've grown so used to this place
The rocky grounds, the sunlight
I lay here in your fields
And it holds me through the night
All the flowers and trees that are filling my sight
I've grown so close to this place, leaving doesn't feel right

But maybe I've just been standing on the beach
Only coming inland in rare times of chance
As if by some miracle your coastline had been breached
And I gladly embrace all the kindness it grants
I feel so safe there with your sandy shores in reach
Lured into your land; have I been in a trance?

Archipelago
I just can't let go
I guess I don't know
If we'll be as I hope
When I have to go
From this place that's home
This place that's home
The archipelago

The architecture of my soul
Is crumbling at the core
My foundation is still sturdy
But I lose balance as I keep building on more

The landscape of my being
Consumed by all the things I'm feeling
When I can't see the things I'm seeing
Is when I feel I've lost the meaning
Oh, I'm sinking
I'm sinking!

My trees go up in flames
My rocks start to crumble
The skies don't look the same
And in come the rain and thunder

Wash over my land!
Strike my barren fields!
Show me all the power
That this wild storm yields!

But I'm just anticipating the storm
In fear of what could lie ahead
I feel these tropical waters
Turning colder as more time passes by

Will I return and just find an ocean?
A wild, wild ocean
I thought you'd be here with me in this ocean
But you left me in wild, wild motion

When I return to our waters
Will your islands still be there?

Or will the plates of earth have shifted?
And I'm stuck here stranded in the sea
When my corals have lost their colors
Will the waters still be fair?
I know that over time we have both drifted
And I hope you'll still be there for me

I just can't let go
I just can't let go
Archipelago
Archipelago

But I guess that maybe that's just how it goes
Land reshapes and disappears
But I'll return to the archipelago
And I'll hope that you're still here

Running in the Night

The sun sets
Lives recess
But I set
Out into the night and I run
To get this weight off my chest

It's so peaceful
Don't have to hold up my guard
I just run through the motionless
And look up at the stars

You fear the night
And what could go wrong in the dark
But I just feel the soothing comfort
Of this lively stillness that brings joy to my heart

See the night sky
And the shape of the silhouette the trees make against it
See the quiet homes
And the shadows they create with the warm light they emit
Feel the cold air
And the way it collides against the warmth of your skin, alive
Hear the silence
And the little breaks in it as a dog barks or a car rolls by

I love the night sky
I love the quiet homes
I love the cold air

I love the silence

And most of all,
I love the little breaks in the silence
You are a break in my silence

HOME, forever (pt. II)

Boxes hovering in motionless space
People around me saying to pick up the pace
And just like the frames on the floor, I'm feeling so out of place
Bodies torn apart as the grounds beneath change
I look up to see a solemn look on your face
And all I want to hear is your voice say it'll all be okay

This will all be okay
This will all be okay
It's okay, it's okay
It's okay, I'm okay

Lost in the motions, stuck in imbalance
I start to notice what, to me, really matters
I don't want to hurt you, I don't want to lose you
I'm trying to adjust, but I fear for the new view

Will it all be okay?
Will it all be okay?
Can I stay? Can I stay?
Will I stay? Every day

As the scales start to tip
My mind starts to shift
I think of the places we've been
Could this all be a gift?
Yes it is, yes it is
And sorrow starts to lift

I don't know what this is
But I'll take what I can get

This has all been okay
This had all been okay
It's okay, it's okay
It's okay, we're okay

This is not my home anymore
This is my home now
But not forever
Someday I'll find myself a new home
A home that I can call my home
My home, forever

If I Wasn't There

Where would you be
If I wasn't there?
Where would you be
If you didn't share?
Where would you be
If I didn't care?
Where would we be
If we weren't there?

A call of distress
To help you out of this mess
And all that it says
In this little text
Is "Can we talk about your brother?
Your friend gave me your number
I don't want to be a bother
A bit of assistance is all that I'm after"

Turns out that wasn't true, but we'll get to that in a little
I do my best to help you, give the advice you need to hear
I think I'm helping, giving the reassurance you are needing
But little did I know, there's another reason why you're here

I thought that would be the end of it
You'd take my words and make your way
But I didn't know 'til now, you hadn't even started it
You still had something left to say
But you didn't quite have the courage yet

Save it for another day

Up all night
Two nights later, 1:19
I just laid there
Watching your heart pop up on my screen
Told me there's someone
But never said it was me
Now you're stuck here
Torn between myself and the enemy

Well, I don't quite mean it like that
But we don't get along well
Nevermind, just ignore that
You tell me the truth, as long as I won't tell
You don't want to start a war
Don't want to end things badly
But if I wasn't there
Where would you be?

We didn't plan for this to happen
I would never have imagined
That we would end up where we are
We were both so scared to start
An awkward circumstance
We got here just by chance
We could have been anywhere
And yet we were there

But if I wasn't there

Would you still be with him?
And if it would have ended
Then when?

I think of all the ways you've changed me
And all the things I'm rearranging
Just so maybe I'll create some space
To fit you neatly into place
I see your lovely glowing face
That no one ever could replace

Within a week, I was hanging out at yours
Sharing music in the kitchen, spilling flour on the floor
Talking 'til we don't know what we're saying anymore
And when it came time to leave, I was left just wanting more

Within a month, I had a poem for you written
You'll get to that one soon enough, just hold on a few more minutes
I let you read it for the first time on March 22nd
You said you loved my words and felt appreciated

Within 2 months, we went on our first official date
We started our journey with a journey 'round the lake
I started getting used to having a smile on my face
And I've got a good feeling that my life's about to change

Within a year, imagine where we both could be
We'd be together and happy still, hopefully
I could be free from all my pain, maybe someday, just eventually
And it could all be so perfect, like it was always meant to be

Where would you be
If I wasn't there?
Where would you be
If you didn't share?
Where would you be
If I didn't care?
Where would we be
If we weren't there?

What lies ahead
Is not very clear
The past in my head
Just leaves me in fear
But now I can see
You're right here, my dear
Wherever we'd be
I'm glad that we're here

IN THE RIVER

Are we just cargo?
on this boat
heading downstream
drifting to the Few Sea

Is this all we know?
words we're told
living in dreams
life is but one of those

How did we lose control?
strength, where'd you go?
I'm not how I seem
but good thing nobody knows

I'm washing away
I'm washing away
I'm washing away
In the river of pain
We're washing away
We're washing away
Growing number each day

The stars are twinkling
Fading out, hard to see
Nothing left to keep me holding on
No way to hold back all my fears

But shouldn't I be relieved?
All my emotions are coming out for you to see
They're coming out my eyes, mouth, and mind
Flowing so violently

I'm worried about where this stream is going
But there's no chance of slowing
So I guess I'll just lay here and follow
Whichever way my emotions are flowing

They're washing away
They're washing away
They're washing away
Hopefully they'll wash away
Maybe someday
Maybe someday
We will all feel okay

No, let's be realistic
This will never go away

This will never go away
It will never flow away
We will never quite feel safe

There's nothing holding me at bay
There's nothing holding me to stay
I'll just keep floating away
In the river
In the river of our pain

Fireworks

Bursts of colored powder, going off like fireworks

Thoughts are getting louder, going off like fireworks

I can't find an answer, gotta find something that works

It's the fact that they'd consider, that's the part that really hurts

—

So inconsiderate
A simple, thoughtless concept
Not yet even brought into fruition
I can't handle it
I just sit here slowly suffering, leading up to the onset
When these are the things that we come up with, should we follow
intuition?

Why does it bother me?
I know it's wrong, but that's not right
Create disturbance, suck up the attention
Why is it that you can't see?
The scene is hung, you stained the sight
Maybe that wasn't your intention

It's going off like fireworks
It's going off like fireworks
I'm going off like fireworks
I'm holding on to dire words
Going off like fireworks

I don't want to lose you because of this
I abused myself because of this
Find another thing to do instead of this
Can you forgive after I said all this?

Sometimes I wish I could let go
But I know in the end I'd be filled with regret so
I stay in the darkness and choose to resent those
Who make shows of their colors; who am I to prevent those?

—

Bursts of colored powder, going off like fireworks

Thoughts are getting louder, going off like fireworks

I can't find an answer, gotta find something that works

It's the fact that they'd consider, that's the part that really hurts

It's the fact that I'd destroy her, that's the part that *really* hurts

Coral Reef

Drifted up at our feet in a bottle
A map with no X marks the spot
An open-ended journey
With no set start, no set stop
Just a chance to find treasure
We might as well give it a shot
The sun starts to set
Are we ready or not?

Although the shore is getting dim
There is life in the rim
We came here on a whim
So into the coral reef we will swim

In the coral reef
In the coral reef
Is love what it seems?
Is it meant to be?

We stay in the reef
And hope to find it right here
Easily within reach
But here in the reef
We hold each other tight, near
Is this love? It's pristine

This place is a nesting ground for our wishes
All of the sorrows we've borrowed will sleep with the fishes

Keep on swimming, this ocean feels endless
Knowing the greatest treasure may lie in the trenches

Though the inner limits may be lifeless
As we head into deeper water
We'll wear this pendant to bring us likeness
And hope it's not an Opal Necklace, Harry Potter

In the coral reef
In the coral reef
If there's love in this sea
I guess we'll just have to see

If we keep diving deeper, we could eventually drown
So do we tread water here, or continue on down?
Living right here, we could live thousands of years
This stable sea bed could save us all our tears
I know through the struggle is where real growth happens
So we can push on through, no matter what happens
It's easy to hide your true self, camouflage like the sea dragons
But I want to look deeper, find the pearl you've held captive

Deep sea love, we lost all our light
The pressure's too much, got no will to fight
You were once my breath, now I'm struggling for air
This water's turned red, but I don't think I care
Is it better to lose than to love
When we can't go far enough?
Is it better to give it all up
Even with as far as we've come?

In the coral reef
In the coral reef
This love can't go deep
It is not meant to be

This love can't go deep
It will drown in this sea

Weapons

We've all got these weapons
God's creation
Create division
A competition
All the wrong intentions
Not to mention
They're given to the children
Pre-parturition

We didn't choose to have these weapons
We just got what we were given
Didn't choose which side we're on, but we must bear them
Our biggest strength, our greatest weakness

We're born with these weapons
The inception
Not much limitation
Our creation
They just follow what you show them
Imitation
We won't follow their direction
Insurrection

Shoot 'em off
Cock it and reload
Have your fun, because we all know, you only live once
Show 'em off
Oh, these kids don't need to know

Don't you know, that you can only lose it once

Resist the temptation
When they try to tell you, don't listen
They can take over your being
Only if you're willing

Put it in the movies!
Glorify it on the big screens!
Want it, love it, need it!
While they're begging on their weak knees!

Put it all over the media!
And then complain how they're mistreating 'ya!
But you do it to yourself
Can't you see the way they're leading us?

Even without these weapons
We can have fun
Creation, destruction
Both of them can
Come from outside and within
Both scarred and fresh skin
Original function
Find the joy from within

We were born with these weapons
Oh, how did it happen?
We will die with these weapons
They're the cages we're trapped in

Dark Skies, Dark Water

Down by the river
Dark skies, dark water
Eager to get going
To release for a moment
My walls become thicker
My tears, they flow quicker
At the thought that you'd do that
Sacrifice the one thing you have
So if you'd please reconsider
This won't make anything better
You're worth more than that
You're too important to me for that
I don't want to be there
But I can't leave you alone 'cause I'm so scared
There are other people in this bayou
And they will take it from you

You don't need it
You don't need it
You can't reseal it
Can't reseal it

Dark skies, dark water
Bodies, uncovered
Free mind, free figure
All lies, my lover

If you ever choose to do it
I would trust that you would tell me
I promise I won't lose it
I want to keep this shoreline healthy
Don't think you're keeping things better by keeping it from me
It's not telling me that would make it worse
We can work it out, understand both sides
No matter how much it may hurt
So when you're thinking this is what you want to be
I'll remind you of your worth to me
And if and when you're drifting through the tides
I'll solemnly wait and hope you're alright
I'll be watching, eyes closed, from the beach's dry land
But before you do, please just remember, I hope you understand
When you're wanting some comfort
Strength and freedom in your form
Just come a little closer
And I will make you feel good

You don't need it
You don't need it
You can't reseal it
Can't reseal it

Dark skies, dark water
Bodies, uncovered
Free mind, free figure
All lies, my lover

You Said It First

You told me that you loved me
But now get mad when I repeat those simple words
Hey, don't get mad at me
You said it first

Time with you feels like a waste
Is that a sign of what we're worth?
Hey, don't get mad at me
You said it first

You tell me that we're ending
But argue with me when I say this won't work
Hey, don't get mad at me
You said it first

I tell you that it's over
'Cause I can't stay here where things just get worse
Go ahead, get mad at me
I said it first

—

I didn't mean to tell you that
I'll take it back when we wake up
I'm just wishing I could take it back
I can't sleep—can't say it if I can't wake up

This is a prison and a war scene
This love is shattered, beat down, cursed
We both know we can't keep forcing
And I don't care who says it first

are WE SAFE?

The stones have settled down
The beach doesn't make its move
We see the people on dry ground
They're each looking down on you
And as you've sat here over time
Your hate for them came through
You want them to help you climb
But there's nothing they can do

Solemnly some still sit
Some are swimming
Some just sink

Melancholy deep s***
Loses meaning
Do you think

That they're taking space ships
Up to the stars
We're reflecting?

Guess we get what we get
That's fine with me
We're all taking it real slowly

But down here in the Few Sea
All we really want is safety
Safety from all that's done wrongly

Down here in the Few Sea
We will try to drift on safely
Drowning ourselves out from hurting
But even down here in the Few Sea
Can we truly live in safety?
Or are we just pretending?
'Cause are we ever really safe?
Are we safe? Are we safe?

We hide beneath an ocean, but few see, few see
We're drowning in emotion, but few see, few see
We're living in slow motion, in the Few Sea, where few see
We can't handle the commotion, in the Few Sea, in the Few Sea

When the waves wash wildly, wind will wreck what was once waking
When we will waste what moments we have waiting, wilting every day
What if we won't wait, we will wash away the wretched water
When we wage war, we'll waste no more

"Put your arms to rest"
They keep saying
On the brink

Weapons grounded, document
The journey
Won't miss a thing

Hold on, wait a minute!
The dot's missing
Line 12's enemy

You know what, I can't take it
Who cares, I just want to keep believing
One day we will see

dnim fo etats a si aes wef eht

~~~

I'll stay right here
Sinking in the Few Sea
'Cause in the cusp of this calamity—
—NO!!!
Returning back to old habits, I see?
NO!!!!!!!!!!!!
YOU DON'T CONTROL ME!!!!!
Oh, yeah?
Then why'd you write all those poems about me?
I heard what you said...
I'M DONE!!!
THERE IS NOTHING!...CAN'T YOU SEE!
...th-th-THERE IS NOTHING I CAN'T BE!!!!
~~~

Where I Was(n't) Found...

You held me there
Where I was found
Lying there
Upon the ground
But who you found
It wasn't me
Your heart, it pounds
Your love for me

This was a war
But I'm the only casualty
Death at my door
And I open it casually
I don't want to hurt you
So don't you come after me
What's there inside me now
It isn't what you'd found in me

So please,
Please leave before I go

The Death of Him

He goes to bed late, so much on his mind
Hasn't had a good night's sleep since who knows when
He looks at his past with hate, wishes he could rewind
He destroys himself with these thoughts, though it could be the death of
him

He feels so insignificant, nothing he does could matter to anyone
He knows his life is just a synonym for all the mistakes he has made
Beats himself up, blasts some music, wakes up in a puddle of tears on the
floor
He knows it could be the death of him, but he'll keep on doing it anyway

He just lays there on the couch, with his head in the cushions
He just lays there in his head, with his heart filled with pushpins
He just waits there with his doubts, he wastes away the good things
He just takes in all they said, though it could be the death of him

He starts to pick up on bad habits; draws on his skin, lowers his rations
He thinks of picking up some tablets; won't go outside, loses his passions
He wants to split himself from the bad thoughts; on the inside, a mental
disconnection
He knows it could be the death of him; knows he has friends, but he's too
scared to message them

He knows it could be the death of him
But no one else is helping him
He just wants life to begin again
But at the same time he is ending it

He screams and he cries
Envies those who have died
He dreams and he tries
Letting go of his pride
Tears stream from his eyes
Until soon, they run dry
He's built walls 'round his mind
Concealing all that he hides
Won't let anyone inside
Believe me, I've tried
When we see, he denies
Says he's doing fine
Tells us he's alright
All lies, all lies
He lives all his life
In perpetual night
There's blood on the knife
He's lost the will to fight

He turns off the lights
Says his goodbyes
Though nobody's there
He hopes the words find them in time
He goes for a drive
Takes a left, takes a right
Pulls off to the side
Ready to give up his life
He jumps
But he flies

And in the sky, he writes
Writes line after line
A poem of hope
A poem of light
He's been broken
But he'll be alright
He survived, he survived

—

Though he reached the sky
The sun still doesn't shine
And the fall from that height
Could destroy him if he can't grow wings in time
I wish there was a way to make things alright
I wish I could kill his fears without letting him die
Maybe he just needs some space and time
And maybe someday he'll be fine
I wish I could save him
I would do anything to save his life
I wish I could save him...
I would do anything to save my life

~~~ (wishy-washy)

We're quite iffy, aren't we?
Barely living, wishy-washy
All our doubts are creeping, haunting
We're just waiting, wishing, wanting

The waves are overtaking, wind still blowing
We've stayed sinking in this ocean, even though we've all been knowing
Our time here's been fine, but now I am realizing
That this is not a good current for me to be riding

Carrying the past, present, and future is way too much weight
I'm so overwhelmed
If only there was someway

Time to make my decision, I'm done with the somedays
Today is today
And today is just one day

Today is today
And today I will escape

Where We Came From \\ rearview

We've come so far from the Few Sea
We've come so far, but still few see
I just hope maybe *you* see
I just hope maybe *you* see

I almost drowned in the Few Sea
I let the sorrow consume me
I just hope maybe *you* see
I just hope maybe *you* see

The river led me to the Few Sea
The Few Sea led me to safety
I just hope maybe *you* see
I just hope maybe *you* see

I've come so far from the Few Sea
I've come so far from where I used to be
I just hope maybe *you* see
I just hope maybe *you* see

I won't forget where we came from
As I walk from the Few Sea
Don't forget where we came from
I just hope maybe *you* see

\\

Even as I walk away
It's almost like I want the pain
Maybe you will never see
Maybe you will never see

Even as I walk away
The rearview tempts my eyes to stay
Maybe I will never see
Maybe I'll never be free

Banana Sandwiches

You're eating a banana sandwich
Telling me how much you love them
I tell you I hate bananas
I haven't eaten one in years
You say I ought to try one of your sandwiches
I guess I'll taste it if I must
You have me try one at your house once
I think I found myself a new love

We don't need your sunshine
We got all the light we need right here
We can have a fun time
We know that this time is free so we're...

Making banana sandwiches
Playing Uno to pass the time
Just vibing in the kitchen
Slow dance to Axel Flóvent, Quiet Eyes

I never thought that things would come to this
I've been smiling more and you notice it, don't ya?
There's always been something I was missing
But I didn't know just how to fix it
Never wanted a relationship
Always thought bananas taste like sh– (Hold up!)
Never knew there was something I so much wanted
But I guess there was and this is it

Like the banana on its sliced bread
Peanut butter in between
With a shake of cinnamon on top
I'm glad I tried you out and got to know ya
Though I had my doubts initially
You know I really like-a you a lot

So we'll make banana sandwiches
And play Uno to pass the time
Make a big mess in the kitchen
Slow dance to Axel Flóvent, Quiet Eyes
I'm glad that I took my chance on this
Didn't know this would feel so right
Imagine all that I'd be missing
Come dance, my heart's all open, this is life!

If I could remind my past self one thing
Right now, the one thing I'd say is:

There are no solid answers, kid
Think of all the things she brought into light
And all that she could still bring, now I say
I'm glad that I got to know ya, let's live live!

>enough.

I found somebody I can love
Whose love is always more than enough
I found someone who can love me
Period, unconditionally

You are more than enough
More than enough
You're more than enough
More than enough

The Harpist

Hey, you've grown so strong
All your scars are living proof
Remember just how far you've come
Please, don't forget why we made you
Everyone is here for you and you for them
Remember how much you are loved, again and again

Just know that when you play your strings
You play for her, you play for me
You play for everyone you meet and everyone who'll ever be
But remember you play for you, most importantly

Whether you live in duet or in symphony
Or simply play your life solo
When your notes sound out of tune or sweetly serene
No matter what, we're here for you

Make a song you're proud of
And share it with the world
You can change it for the better
That's the power of a girl

Like you shape the melody
With just your hands
You shape the future
You change everything; the world expands

I want you to know how important you are
Though you're just a girl and have so much doubt
It takes time to learn how to follow your heart
But you're our whole world and you'll figure it out

Safe with us, your song will never die

bGloaLCDk

My darkness is infused with gold

numb

I sat you down here with me on this chair
Friends all around as the sun takes its leave, truth or dare
Never have I ever felt quite this close to anyone
You lay yourself across my lap and I feel myself start getting numb

Campfire memories, soft conversation
I can't feel anything, but my hand on your waistline
As it gets colder you draw yourself closer 'til your body holds me tight
I'll warm the blood in your veins while your legs are numbing mine

I'll stay right here 'til I go numb, but that's alright
You don't have to move a muscle, I'll stay here all night
Don't worry if you're hurting me, I'll be just fine
I'll savor the flavor of this ache in my young mind

Your bone on my skin, pain thrown to the wind
I'll hold you within, I won't pull the pin
When you're around me, I feel my heart pounding
As long as you're happy, I'd go numb for you gladly

Even when my back's about to break
I don't want you changing, have your way
I'll keep a smile on my face and mask the pain
Even if I need an amputation, that's okay

There's no way I would leave as my whole body goes numb
The feeling of you here is too good to let go of

Colder

Spending time with you doesn't feel like it used to
I know they say beauty lies in the eyes of the beholder
But it's so hard for me to hold you
When there's no color in the picture

You let me speak to the sky
Then lay your head on my shoulder
Don't let the feelings reply
Will it be like this when we're older?

I hold on to what was
I've become such a hoarder
Your heart is warmed up
While mine just gets colder

I'd like to ask you some questions
But I know the answers already
Our minds live in different dimensions
I think our time here is ending

We once had bright flames
And like portraits of our ancestors
I put our time in its frames
As I watch it smolder

You'd let me speak until I die
With your head laid on my shoulder
Now the feelings can't hide

We won't be like this when we're older
We won't be like this for much longer

Hyperspace

I'm scared of the high
Because I'm scared of the fall
I'm not scared to die
But of losing it all

You gave me your all
And I won't let that die
I think I'm ready to fall
So please take me high

*

Shantel is awesome. La-la-la-la-la...

*

I'm ready to fall
I'm ready to fall
I'm ready to fall
I'm ready to fall

. . .

I'm risking it all
I'm risking it all

. . .

You're the one who I call
When I'm ready to fall

. . .

I'm ready to fall

I'm ready to fall
I'm ready to fall
I'm ready to fall

*

How difficult could it be?

*

Alive and free
(That's what she did to me)

Alive and free
(That's what you did to me)

Kepler-47

Two suns
But you're the star
Far out dust
Pulls you apart
From the inside out
You go through ups and downs
But through it all you're proud
Of this new ground you found
A whole world of your creation
Always growing, always changing

But not far off
In the same galaxy
Two worlds got lost
But for now they don't see

That their paths have crossed
They've started their story
But as time ticks and tocks
Their orbits rarely meet

Rock strikes rock
These worlds are now colliding
Is this our shot?
Is this another 303 meets 50?

And that's where you come in
Though she started this story

You were there all along
The seams in this book, the very atoms of our being

And now we're here and I thank you
For helping me do this more easily
For being a friend and a comfort
In this time of new discovery

Kepler-47
Come teach me a lesson
Help me make these worries lessen
Bring to life the light I've never shone
I know the ways you're testing me
And all the ways you're helping, please
Pull me with your gravity
And bring me to the habitable zone

At the core, a heart of gold
Emitting yellow rays of light
Over all this time, not a lie you've told
Not a dimming in your brightness

Even in the middle of a crisis
You've always got strength and such insight
You can trust I truly trust you
Would it be wrong to say you're always right?

Too close to your fire
Has threatened to burn out others
That's when my sky fills up

With comets and meteor showers

I'll be the one
The one to take what I have now
And leave the light that I've exhausted
To burn in the shadows

She'll see the suns
See them both for what they are
And no matter how the light's refracted
Never tends to stray too far

Off-center from my own home star
Time knows no rival, but only goes so far
I know it'll have to get better, get better because we'll be
Sharing the light, the light of two suns

In this system
I've done a lot of resisting
But we work it through together

I'll go with them
The closer I get, the farther I'm drifting
But I promise "I'll do better"

And now I move out
No longer in that zone
But you'll adjust to it now
Extend your reach until this feels like home

Kepler-47
Come teach me a lesson
Help me make these worries lessen
Bring to life the light I've never shone
I know the ways you're testing me
And all the ways you're helping, please
Pull me with you gravity
And bring me to the habitable zone

I'm blue, while she's pure, illuminous, opal white
One can't see my light, even in the darkest of nights
But you lend your light, reflect just right
Extend my sight, make it all alright
No need to hide, inside
Don't fight, your crime is not defined
By the judge inside your head
By the things that people said
Hold tight, breathe, just take in the view
4-7-8, you're okay, I'll always be here for you
But now it is time, it's all up to you
To practice the words that you want to recite
To silence the voice that you know just sells lies
Ignite the light inside that's right
You'll be fine, rewrite, rewrite, rewrite
Don't open your closest to closing wounds now
You'll only go slower, sink lower, miss out

Kepler-47
Come teach me a lesson
Kepler-47

Come teach me a lesson

She's says, "Come lay with me by the water
The waves aren't coming for you, I swear
I'll let the earth hold you tight
I won't make you talk but I will listen if you'd like"

I don't want the comfort
Just let me lay here in the rough
I try to compensate for my shortcomings
It just is never quite enough

I know the clouds go on forever
But the sun's still shining through
And when I think about this curious weather
I know the star up there is you

Suck me into the sun
Engulf me in the fire
I'd rather be there than down here
Where I'm slowly cutting wires

The place of healthy habitation, I've been there before but not routine
I just lay there in frustration, 'cause I can't bear it when I stray
You try to balance the equation, I feel better about where we'll go and
where we've been
I need us all to just be patient, and one day I'll be there to stay

I'll be there forever
If you say that it's okay

Back At The Lake ||| Ducks

We're back at the lake
To see the place I promised I'd take you to
Got the essentials but not much plan
Just a time to give thanks, a celebration of two
But we could stay out here forever
Even without much to do
We both just need each other
Because you love me and I love you

We just got here and already I'm slipping up
Stepping into holes and tripping all over myself
I see the others who just laugh but then remember you; you've got my
back
And then I don't feel so bad; I can't do that to you; I've got your back

Taking our time at the shorelines of our lake
Overlooking all the water from above and all the life that lies in its waves
And even as the sun goes does, we'll stick around
We'll stick around, this life we found, we'll stay for now, at this lake we've
walked around

5 to 1, you
How the tables have turned
After all I've won, true
This is what you have earned

We'll share our words in the old stone gazebo
Spell out my tracklists by memory

Dancing and smiling, as you hold me so close
You don't know how much that meant to me

Even as the spiders start to creep in and surrounds us
And other people interrupt us; Mike and Ikes
We can always come back even though we're leaving now
We'll take the lake along back with us; tonight, for life

Your card
How fancy it was
Your creation
Your words
A reply to my own

My pleasure to see
It means to much to me
Take it all in
Cures some of my worst
Our time, not alone

And I left it behind
When we returned back to yours
Just hang around for a while
Your heart in my chest
But I didn't know, I didn't know

I go back when I notice
Though it's late and my fuel is running low
A promise of reconstruction
But we all know the original is always best

All the words you wrote, so good to know

Taking our time at the shorelines of our lake
Overlooking all the water from above and all the life that lies there in its
waves
And when the sun comes back around, we'll reclaim our ground
It'll stick around, this life we found, though we can't stay for now, we hold
this lake in our hearts with every pound

But even when we're there, we still haven't touched its water
We stay on the ground, around the lake, still hear its sound
We still feel its waves, this is just the beginning, I'm so glad I brought her
Next time we'll go out, though we know many have drowned, this life we
made is so profound, I hope we stick around

| | | | | | | | | | | | | | | | | | | | | | | | | | | | | | | | | | | | | | | | | | | | | | | | | | | | | | | | | | | | | | | | | | | | | | | | | | | | | | |

Your strength leads me like ducks in a line
Though I stray from your direction from time to time
I'll return before too long because, aligned with you, I feel so nice
It truly makes me glad that I am alive
I know I don't have all my ducks in a row
My mind can break off course like Jeff, you know
You make a path and I will follow
I won't forget about myself though
I still need you to see my needs
'Cause this relationship has two sides
But right now, I think I need you to lead as you clear out the reeds
And whatever you need me to do, I will abide

I believe, though sometimes it's hard, your way is right
Won't have all my issues and can hold them back on my own
Right now we'll work these things out together and I will hold you so
tight
Your ducks will lead me home

Out On The Lake --- Steps

On the tenth day of June
We made it two months as two
Spent some time in the water
I did it all just for you

Then we head out to a new lake
We drove down for your birthday
With a few friends and your family
Why does my mind always think worst case?

I can't see you like this
Can't see you like you want me to
You won't see me like this
No matter how much I want you to

I'm out on the lake, but too scared to touch its water
My doubts and mistakes won't let me be pulled under
The skin 'round your waist takes the smile from my summer
I live in a place where to swim is to suffer

—

So I paddle alone
I just drift to and fro
While you all have a good time
I know I should be there too, shouldn't I?

A crane swoops in
A sign
A change for something better
I am out on the lake
But still
I have never touched the water

I choose to spend time in my mind
While you spend your time with those you love
I wish that I could change your mind
But I'm still too scared to open up

Finally I look up in your direction
You have a trick you want to show me
But I can't look long 'cause you're too different from me
Thinking like this, I'll always be lonely

I was out on the lake, but I never touched its water
My doubts and mistakes wouldn't let me dive under
The skin 'round your waist took the smile from my summer
I live in a place where to swim is to suffer
I live in a place where to drown is to love her

—

When it's time to go, you pack your stuff in the car
I just sit in my seat and tear myself apart
She gave me her phone, so I could listen to music
I hate that you do this, I hate that I'm useless
Though we're two feet apart, it feels like you're so far away

It's like my Soul's in New York, in a whole different state
While you're a Billion miles away, still here in this car
And my Condition will fray, because I'm Human at heart

I know it's not over yet
I know that you love me
I hope it's not over yet
I hope you still love me

This was not our lake
We'll be okay
This was not our lake
We'll be okay

- -

I'm taking steps to close the gap
Between us, get us back on track
Together, where we should be at
Don't ever want to hold you back

I called you that night on the phone
And explained why I'd stayed all alone
The water cuts me to the bone
But I know I'll need it if I want to grow

I walked and we talked for over an hour
You're the strongest of beasts but you've chosen a coward
I don't want you to change, but I don't want to suffer
I live in a place where to drown is to love her

But I'm taking steps
To show
That I love her

7 a.m.

I want to be with you
at 7 a.m.
Up on the rooftop,
watching the sunrise;
much more than friends
Your eyes to the sky
My eyes locked on you
Your cold hands in mine
I'll warm them for you
I don't want to come down
Feel the hope in the dew
If you got lost in the clouds
I'd never want skies of blue

Hopewell

I've been living on this cliffside
For a while not knowing one day I'd have to go down
Into the water I never thought would reach me
Though the tides may rise and fall
I feel my size, I'm not that tall
Who knew I'd one day be here?
I guess you all did all along
Is it my time to risk it all?

The static friction's got me stuck
I ease in a bit, but not enough
I'll take a chance, I'll push my luck
And hope that then something will budge
There's no easy way to get over the hump
You just get there on a whim
So just throw me in or let me jump
And I will learn to swim

It's not enough, I'm not enough
I'll try my best, I'll take the plunge
It's not enough, I'm not enough
I'll try my best, if you will trust

Hopewell, hopewell
I don't know if it will go well, go well
But there is no tell–, no telling
How this will end well, and well
If I screw this up then oh well, oh well

Then you all can send help, send help
I'll just hope, well I'll just hope
We'll never know until I go
I'll just hope, well I'll just hope
We'll never know until I go

I want the freedom but also the struggle
You don't think I can take it and say
You can't lose hope if you start to stumble

Well, hope is my best friend
I think I just need to jump
And see how this will end

I don't know if I will do it right
But if I'm given the chance
I'll find my way over time

I know I won't do it right
But neither did you
And I want to try my best

I'll find my way
I'll make you proud
I'll put my limits to the test

A Demonic Love Note

What are we doing here
If it's not to enjoy it?
All the moments we make
All the moments not wasted
We have a chance
We have a chance and we take it
I've got my fear
I've got my fear and I'll face it

Tiptoe, tiptoe
Go slow, stay low
Make a run for it now
And don't regret it somehow

I won't regret it, I won't regret it
I found my border, and I met it
You met me there, and we crossed it
I had my fear, but I lost it
You took my fear, and you tossed it

A tipped over peak
Lying there in the street
Pick it up and we leave
An uplifting weight in our feet
A stop at the park
To brush on our art
Leave it in front of his yard
With his name, a face, and some hearts

Tiptoe, tiptoe
Let's go, let's go!
Looking back toward it now
I don't regret it, I'm proud

I don't regret it, I don't regret it
I found my border, and I met it
You met me there, and we crossed it
I had my fear, but I lost it
You took my fear, and you tossed it

No one knows it
But our faces show it
We'll never tell
I know it, you know it
We know it well
This life is hell
A paradise if we grow it
Maybe someday we will tell
Maybe someday we will tell

DAYorDREAMING

I just woke up from a long, long nap
And I'd do anything to bring you back
I know you're probably not that far
But I can feel it pulling at my heart

Is it day or am I dreaming?
Are we okay or are you leaving?
These thoughts of mine, always competing
But when you're here, (truly here) you give it meaning

It's 2 a.m.
And I should be sleeping
But every night that I spend alone
I get caught daydreaming

Once I leave your arms
A depression takes over my being
It lasts all through the night and the next day
It won't stop until evening

I screwed up again
My mistakes keep repeating
Though in different forms each time
These issues, it feels like there's no chance in beating

This is who I am
And I know I'm changing
But every time I see your face

I'm sorry that I keep you waiting

Is it day or am I dreaming?
Am I okay or am I bleeding?
These words of mine, have lost their feeling
But when you're here, (truly here) you give it meaning

In the daytime
I just want to see your face
You've been running while I've been crawling
Don't think I'll ever catch your pace

When I'm dreaming
It feels like I've already lost you
Your edges kind of vague
Your eyes are quicksand I could fall through

The more I struggle
The more I'm sinking
I reached out for your arm
But what was I thinking?

I just pulled you down
But you refused to sink
When I hit my lowest
You reached your peak

When I first fell in
I should have just relaxed
Let you be yourself

But it's too late to go back

I know I hurt you last night
I hate it when I make you cry
I just keep pushing more and more
Until you make me say goodbye

—

It's not like you to not be right here
But I guess that's all my fault
It's not like you to show any fear
But I guess that's what I taught

Just now replying to your text
Because I didn't know how to say it best
But I'm sorry that I made this mess
And I hate nothing more than to see you stressed

Is it day or am I dreaming?
Are we okay or are you leaving?
These thoughts of mine, always competing
But when you're here, (truly here) you give it meaning

An airplane flies across
Through the dip in the trees
It carries hope that it offers
But I can't hold onto its speed
I look back down
The overpass passes over

It's not as high as I thought
But it still elevates the others

I just woke up from a sleepless nap
And I want you here, I've got your back
Let me know when you are fine
You can come on over, I'll give you all my time

:

Elizabeth

I went for a walk with Elizabeth
She told me how she really lived
And how she doesn't fear her death
'Cause she'll be proud of everything she did

I had a talk with a girl named Rose
She asked me: What is it that everybody knows?
We'll all die someday but for now we live
So give everything in this world all the love you can give

I had a chat with a man downtown
He told me there's no way around
All the things I want are straight ahead
And when that road gets rough, don't let the final words be said

I spent some time with John last night
He said that he's missed out a lot in life
Missed chances and fun, lost friends and family
The last thing he said: Don't let yourself end up like me

I'll always remember that quiet day
When a stranger gave her words to me
She stepped in beside me and just talked away
And I'm so glad she did and gave my path new meaning
Because Elizabeth, she did it, she really lived
And I'll do it too, I'll live my life
Living life alive, no words unsaid
Thank you for your time, my friend, Elizabeth

Falling Still

You called me up in the dead of night
And asked if I would like to talk
You could tell that I felt dead inside
And hung up before I could say a word

All I wanted was to be held tight
And have someone to accompany me on a walk
Who would tell me things will be alright
But you hung up before I could say a word

You are the moon and I am the tide
You come around and I lose the desire to hide
But before long, the sun comes, and you go away
And now you're gone, I'm undone, and recede to the waves

Sometimes I love you
I'm just too scared to say it
Sometimes I want to
My lips can't be persuaded

—

I called you up in the dead of night
But couldn't find the strength to talk
You asked if I was doing alright
But I hung up before you said another word

You called me back in the blink of an eye
And said you think about me a lot
I struggled to speak as I started to cry
I think I mumbled "I love you," I hope you heard

I woke up the next morning to a message from you
Just four simple words, "I love you too"
I set my phone down and then cried again
But this time they were tears of letting happiness win

I hold your heart in my hands
Taken out for me
I had a feeling but no matter what, I couldn't shake it
Now I've gotta be careful so I don't trip and fall and break it

—

It's been many months and we've fallen in love
Where once there was silence, words are bubbling up
I was empty, but you filled me up
But now I am scared that it's still not enough

You were always there, always lended your hand
But we all know things never quite go as planned
And lately I've been feeling like I'm falling out of love with you
You hold my clothes in your arms
I'd never want to do you harm
But I think that it's best if I just break up with you

I'm falling apart
You're still falling in love

I'll stop calling your phone
And stop calling this love

I don't want to hurt you
But blood must have blood

Your love cut me open
But now I'm stitching it up

Sea Heart

I got to know you
Inside my dreams
Our love is so true
Or so it seems
I've gotten so used
To my heart's new beat
I won't even notice
As it starts to bleed

I've tried to show you
But you still don't see
If I try to see this through
It could be the death of me
What if all I've ever done
Turns out to be something I'll have to repeat?
What if all that I've become
Is just a ghost of all I'll ever be?

I used to dream of the day that you would talk to me
But now I'm wishing you wouldn't and that you would just leave
I've been swimming, tryna bridge the gap between you and me
My heart's been consumed by the sea

But I still love you
Through the cracks, your light comes through
And over time, I've become you
Just so maybe you'd be mine

Your darkness embracing
All the shame that I'm facing
But there's no way I'm replacing
You now after all this time

I still remember the day that you finally talked to me
But now I'm wishing you hadn't and that I would just leave
I've been sinking tryna bridge the gap between you and me
My heart's been consumed by the sea

This sea's freezing over
And I'm seeking for cover
I can't breathe in this water
Darling, are you a lover?

You're such a beautiful dancer
And a cute take-a-chance-er
I've loved you like a brother
But darling, are you a lover?

Please,
Just give me an answer

I used to dream of the day that you would talk to me
But now I'm wishing you wouldn't and that you would just leave
I've been swimming whichever way the waves are sending me
My heart's been consumed by the sea

All this time I thought that you were falling
But now you step away and I can see
All along it's just been me
I've been alone in this wild sea, swimming foolishly

All this love I've shown
Was it returned wrongly?
Your heat is still haunting
Even as we drift apart

And I'm left alone
I'm still falling
No sense of belonging
I have a wounded sea heart

Neanimorphia

[Pt. I]

You wouldn't hurt a child, right?
So why would you do it to yourself?

You wouldn't neglect a child, right?
So why would you do it to yourself?

You wouldn't let a child say that
So why would you say it yourself?

You wouldn't let a child do that
So why would you do it yourself?

You wouldn't leave a child alone, right?
So why do you do it all yourself?

You wouldn't let a child suffer
So why do you neglect your health?

You wouldn't let a child drink that
So why do you drink it yourself?

If all the colors start to fade
You'd bring them all back for a child, right?

;

The worth of youth is priceless
So why would you trade it for some wealth?

Your life's your own, it's timeless
You don't have to be anyone else

You fill your sights with neon lights
They burn so bright that you could melt

I wish I knew what to tell you
To reconnect you with yourself

You waste away your future
Because they wasted all your youth away

You say your past self was a loser
But could you ever say that to her face?

You wouldn't do that to a child, right?
So please don't do it to yourself

Look back upon the path you've paved
Though you've grown, you're still so childlike

—

[Pt. II]

This is why it hurts so much to see
When you do the things you do
I know you're not a child anymore
But that's still how I see you
Don't do that to yourself
Because I see you as her
You wouldn't do that to a child
I know that much for sure

She's still there
And always will be
Beneath your skin
That's why it kills me

We are everyone who we'll ever be
All at once, in this moment
You appear younger than you are to me
You're still eight, though you've kept growing
Go take a look inside the mirror
At the one you've left unnoticed
And when she reaches out her fingers
Please, take her hand and hold it

See You Again

I drove in to Walgreens
You were waiting for me
You walk up and start talking
So casually
I look around
For means of repair
You look at me
For love that's not there
You try to find a way in
I try to find a way out
If I let you win
You may never fade out
I just needed some tape
But I can't even find it
Could you give me some space?
Could you give me some silence?
You ask what I'm here for
I tell you the truth
You say, "I know where that is
I'll get it for you"
We walked out to the parking lot
You asked me to spend the night with you
I said I had other places to go
But I just wanted to get home so I lied to you
You made me so uncomfortable
I hope I never have to see you again
But you helped me out along my search
So I guess it was a good thing in the end

So( )lo(w)

When I leave you solo
I know you feel so low
To be a good friend
I wish I knew how but I don't know

I remember you bought me that CD
After the great storm
I remember you bought me that hoodie
And dang that thing's been worn

You lent me your soul through texts that you sent
Light up my heart and my screen
You've always been there for me as a friend
Since back when I was fourteen

But what do I give in return?
How has your friendship been earned?
Your kindness isn't what I deserve
I feel so bad to the point that it hurts

I know I hurt you when I don't reciprocate
But still you keep a smile on your face
I remain stagnant and wish I could change
If I cry enough tears, will my fears ever wash away?

Maybe someday, I can be there for you
In the way you really want

Maybe someday, I will be there for you
But by then you may be gone

If you left me solo
I know I'd feel so low
But I'm not a good friend
So I wouldn't yell out, "please, don't go"

So(u)l[e]

You should know you're bright
Like a solar flare
Inside your soul
There is so much there
You inspire me
So don't you dare
Send your life down, spiraling
I know it's tiring
But you're not your sole defender
I'll help defend forever
And please don't you ever
Feel like you burden me
I've been there too
I always feel inferior and each day it's worsening
And I feel like all my flaws
Are overflowing, drowning others
I just clench my jaw
Always knowing, but doubting the words
I don't doubt that you care
I hope that I'm always there
By your side, in your mind
I'll be there if you let me be
Sometimes I let fear get the best of me
So I push you away, for days upon days
But when I think back, I think back regretfully
Because you don't deserve that
You're the sun and you send me your energy
And in return you don't ask me for anything

And though I can't be a sun yet, I'll try to be a moon
I'll take in all the light you cast, and reflect some back to you

Bounceback

Remember when I got upset at those words that I saw
And now my tears hang upon everyone's walls
Ruining the moment has always been one of my faults
But I ruin much more than that, I ruin it all

I wish I could go back and tell me to get it together
Don't let little ruined moments ruin your life forever
It's okay for you to cry every once in a while
But don't let the tears ever wash away your smile

I cried on the front lawn until my eyes ran dry
Then screamed at myself through the rest of the night
I pushed myself down to my lowest of lows
But I'll always bounce back no matter how far I go

—

Remember when I shut myself off from you
I didn't respond to your texts for a month or two
So I could see just how much I'd really miss you
And now I know I'll never want to be without

You got so close I had to push you away
'Cause when I get too close to someone, I get afraid
I know now you're no one that I'd ever hate
I just needed some time to figure it out

I'm sorry if I ever caused you to cry
Or stay up all night just wondering why
I pushed you away 'til you were left all alone
But I'll always bounce back no matter how far I go

—

Remember when I came at you for the image that you mouthed
We fought 'til I was lying, crying on the ground
To get out all the animosity built up between us over time
Maybe anger isn't something we should ever hold inside

We've been at war for our whole lives, but now that time in life is over
We're all still kids in the inside, but in our minds we've both grown older
Now I think it's fair to say that I'd consider you my best friend
And that will never happen again, I swear, that was the end

If you cry out for help, I'll be right by your side
In a night with no stars, I will bring you some light
I pushed you, you pushed back, I left you no room to grow
But I know you'll bounce back, you're stronger than you know

c l o s e / distant

When I'm close to you
Feels like it's pulling us apart
And when we're distant
Feels like it's bringing us together

Inequate

Why won't you wear it?
The colors that we share
The only times you wear it
In your bed and here with me

I brought you up
I wrote a song
I gave you my words
And I thought you'd sing along

I love you, I love you, I love you, I do
I want to, please come through, I love you, it's true

Are you embarrassed? Do you hate it?
You say you love it, you're so careless
We share this, I wear it, standing proudly to the public
We talk behind each other's backs but sleep stomach to stomach

You brought me back
Where I belong
You heard my words
But you didn't sing along

I love you, I love you, I love you, I do
I want to, please come through, I love you, it's true
That sweet tune I made you, it holds true for you
If I were to tell you what I've gone through, would you?

So I go hide away in an icy cave
Your warm perimeter's so far away
And I won't return, I might hurt for the rest of my days
I'll remain melting, unsettled, as you inequate

idk. i'm sorry.

I know, I know, I know, I think that this was wrong
I don't know, I don't know, I don't know, don't know who I am anymore

I don't want to be alive right now
I don't want to be around
I feel so bad for what I've done to you
I feel like I can't face you now the same

I know, I know, I know, I know I took it too far
It could have been so positive, instead it's bringing us apart

You seem pretty fine with it, but I'm not okay, I feel so bad
I did something I shouldn't have done to you and I can't handle that

When the suns find out, what will they say?
I'm scared to know
Will they tease or will they condemn?
Can I ever make amends?

I took the touch
I broke the barrier
I stopped the silence
She took the fruit that I was handing her

I felt like cussing
But that's a cheap way to express the pain I'm feeling

I hate myself
I hate this
I don't hate you
I hate what I've done

One hundred days have come and gone

I can't take this back
But of course I would if that was possible

I don't know if this will be okay
Can you ever forgive me?
I kind of think you already have
But I can never be sure, maybe one day I'll see

All I can do right now
Because I don't want it to be over
I want to fix this up in time
Is just take this mistake
And learn from disgrace
And trust that over time we'll work this out
I don't know what I'm doing, I'm just so sorry
For everything I've done, everything I'll do
That I should not have done
I'll make it up to you

—

When you walk out of your room
You say, "I'm all tied up in one big knot"

And I ask, "Can it be fixed?"
And to that you reply with "I don't know"

Well, what did I expect?
We broke the rules and we paid the price
Now, in retrospect
I should have never let you stay the night

—

I don't know how you seem so fine already
Continue on like all is normal
In your mind, was none of this an issue?
Is it a happy story when you tell it?
'Cause I know for me, that's not the way it goes
It wasn't all that bad, but I feel guilty
Maybe it's a good, successful story that just doesn't have a happy ending
And it's depressing

Chapter 3:
EIGHTEEN, pt. II

July 21, 2021 — December 31, 2021

^ • < –

Kepler-47, Pt. II, Ch. 1: Rogue

I've gone rogue
From all I've known

Darkened tones
And brittle bones

Borrowed both
With no return

But I've gone rogue
With no return

—

Hearts of coal
Minds of stone

I can't face it
All alone

Can't kill a ghost
In six months' time

Sea is dry
Be what you like

—

Call me up
The sky-filled sun

All of us
No who, no what

Compassionate
With open hearts

See me now
Be what you like

Kepler-47, Pt. II, Ch. II: A Star Is Born

Caught within a cloud of dust
That's all I am: a cloud of dust
And here you are, I've come so far
One day I will be the star

Way back then I had the guts
But here and now, she calls the cuts
Gathered dust from near and far
'Cause one day I will be the star

Turbulent and open-minded
Over time I've refined it
Knots of gas have since collapsed
I self-attract, I've earned this mass

—

Behind my back, you talk it down
Don't know who to trust in now
Rising up but caught in tar
One day I will be the star

More and more I trust myself
A flash of color in a grayscale cell
Why stop now? I've come this far
One day I will be the star

Who I'll be, not who I was
Without me there can't be us
My core heats up, dust turns to form
That is how a star is born

Kepler-47, Pt. II, Ch. III: Transit

Bright pink
Bright blue
Deep thinking
Turns deep maroon
Put my hands across my face
I'm lost in outer space
In my own embrace
I'm a disgrace

And you carry me, carry me, carry me out
And I can't bear to look
But you're there for me, there for me, here for me now
And I can't bear to look

I sink
Into
Everything
Turns deepened blue
But every time I'm left behind
I can't decide which side you're on
But all along you've been here
Been the truth

And you carry me, carry me, carry me out
And I can't bear to look
But you're there for me, there for me, here for me now
And I can't bear to look

Oh, you're sarcastic
But I'm past it
You won't relapse if
I can clear my vision
And I'll make that decision
'Cause all along you've been here
Seen the truth

A planet was damaged in transit
But somehow I've managed to stand it
I come back
Though nothing turns out how I planned it
I might have learned to love the aftermath

And you carry me, carry me, carry me out
And I can't bear to look
But you're there for me, there for me, here for me now
And I can't bear to look
Brought back
Down to
Earth
Open
My eyes
Arms pulled back
Now gold shines through
I look up to see your face
A transit, lunar phase
The flaws I embrace
Reflect my grace

Kepler-47, Pt. II, Ch. IV: Goodnight.

Sun rises
Red, orange, pink
Rolling white clouds
Softening the scene
Time flies in
My roots are soft and green
But you help me grow
With a single yellow beam

Stand tall
My shadow's missing
High above
But correlating
Afternoon
The wind is changing
Back too soon
A storm is brewing

My mind is a black hole
My mind is a black hole that you let yourself be pulled into
You're kind and reliable
You're kind and reliable and that's why I open up to you

—

My mind is a black hole
My mind is a black hole that you let yourself be pulled into
You're kind and reliable
You're kind and reliable and that's why I open up to you

When the sky exploded
The constellations shifted
Gravity pushed back, a weight was lifted
The good night lies in your sky now
But I might always keep my eyes down
I might always keep my eyes down

I'll see your light again tomorrow
Goodnight.

You thought

I bet you thought your life would get better
But now you're sitting on a plane
Life can only be uphill from here on out
But you're sinking down against the rise in altitude
You did it again...

So close, so close, or so you thought
There's two sides to every story but I don't know which one's mine or not
Am I the one who wouldn't have fought?
Or the one who would have made a fuss of something insignificant?

—

Well, f***
You found a solution
Which is something I should thank you for doing
But I just sound the pollution
Why must I always be choosing?
Can I please just live without intrusion?

It had all been going so well
It was a point to prove how far you've come
You thought you were only moving forward
Well, now you're on your way back to where you came from

Oh no, oh no, you missed your shot
We could forever live in glory and I thought that I was ready
But I guess that I'm still not

I don't want to lose what I've got
But to get all that you have, I'd quickly give it all away
So please save me a spot

—

What's the point in sharing it with her too?
I'll face it on my own, I'll get myself through

—

So close, so close, or so you thought
Oh no, oh no, you missed your shot
So close, so close to what you want
Go home, your home is where you'll start
That's where you'll find her heart

For Now It Keeps Her Sad

You stand there feeling sad and small
And wonder if they care at all
They judge, don't share, overlooking that you're there
A give and take
A heart will break
Their 'friendship' is your last mistake
Moving on, you find his arms
Outstretched with the comfort that you need
Kinds words, a smile
And all the while, a bandage for the bleed

She holds her tear on the tip of her finger
Hold it there and let the feelings linger
Look into it like an introspect-reflecting mirror
Let it soak in right there as you draw it nearer

Your glitter down my left side, got no balance
But you're shining bright to me in the night, like Aurora Borealis
You continue to repeat it, keep it as is
And tell me all the ways they hurt you; aren't we already past this?

—

You're my jewel, but you lost your gem
Claim you'll never get it back again
But I see it in the cracks
As a matter of fact, you never lost it
You were just hiding it from me; I almost lost it

But maybe you're just like me
And you let the sadness stick around just so I would stick around
You just want my warm arms around you
So you let the pain surround you too

One day you will move on
One day I'll look down and you'll be gone
But for now it keeps her sad
So I will hold her close, like we're all we've ever had

Broken Snakes

Sat here on the platform
To get solace you asked for
You got issues, well that's sure
But still create so pure

These twigs that you adorn
With cracks in their S-form
But you're still so insecure
So they went premature

So proud of what you made
And your loss brings so much pain
But though you hide out under gray planks
Through your tears you'll be okay

Oh, you
I see your beauty
In their beauty
In the beauty you create

Through you
I see the few things
That bring cruelty
And the reasons that they break

It's more than you can take

—

Leaves 'round the stick, you're
Sorry for what you did, sure
Keep adding on more
But then stop to help her

Poor kid, you're just so torn
Like the snakes that you still mourn
Because you took the wrong detour
When these floodgates outpoured

So proud of what he made
And we can know that to this day
The leaves still remain and you're okay
But they will not forever stay

He sees it, he's sorry
He means it, not hardly
If he makes a new one
Could that make it up some?
It won't be the same but
I know love will come
Make two into one
Hey, wouldn't that be fun?
He tries hard to fix it
Puts his heart and soul in it
This moment is relived
So can you please forgive?

Oh, you
I see your beauty
In their beauty
In the beauty you create

Through you
I see the few things
That bring cruelty
And the reasons that they break

It's more than you can take

—

It's more than you can take
It's more than you can take
Like a tower in an earthquake
Like the power that a kings gains
Like the thoughts that keep me awake
When too much piled on from today
As if they'll never quite go away
You always come
Crashing down
Trapping out
All the creatively weaved happiness you make

When I feel the need to seethe my fight in you
And there's nothing you or I could ever do
I will just remember those little snakes
Those little broken snakes

Holding Her // The Archer

I hold her dead in my arms
The archer waits in the clouds
We all stand still in the sounds
'Til the beat crashes down
Why do we ignore the alarms?
Our ending anticipated by the onlooking crowd
And just as I'm ready to let her down, here and now
He's ready to shoot me down

Oh, regret
Sweet, sweet regret
Eat, eat you get
To chew on the past
Make the memories last
But when you think of the best
All your hear are the words
Echoing all the worst
And you know it gets better
But it's too late to reset her
It's as if you've always been cursed
The archer's been waiting above
Since I first picked her up
And I know
Although it all hurts so much
I'm making this up
But I'm not

//

Gock, and it's shot
Stop, it's a lot
Like every thought that I'm not all that I thought
I was haunts me, I fought so hard that I lost
Me, "*You got what you want, so why are you not*
Happy? We thought you were ready but now see you're not
You can't hold her with those arms
Shaking like they'll just fall off
Think of all the joy she's brought
But with you her joy just seems to rot"

Shrill screams in the backdrop
On my block in the back lot
Oh, it's hot, take your top off
Take it all off
Okay, stop, put it back on
That was too far
Back in the car
Back it up, in the school lot
Backseat love, oh, it's so hot
Sweat it off, not enough
Toss the glove, not enough
Not enough, not enough
Not enough, not enough
Give it up, give it up
I'm giving up, I'm giving up
I can never give enough...

Oh, regret
Sweet, sweet regret
Eat, eat you get
To chew on the past
Make the memories last
But when you think of the best
All you hear are the words
Echoing all the worst
And you know it gets better
But it's too late reset her
It's as if you've always been cursed
The archer's been waiting above
Since I picked her up
And I know
Although it all hurts so much
I'm making this up
So I'll stop

When you say I'm beautiful

I don't believe it
But I know you mean it
And you don't just say it 'cause you want to
You say it 'cause it's true

Brunette Girl, White Mustang

It's getting late
I've got a lot on my mind
Lookie, blonde mate
Looking nice, enjoy your ride
Brunette girl; white Mustang
What're you doing by my side?
You wanna race?
But if not that's just fine

We head down Gage
I've gotta leave you behind
Still I contemplate
What were you doing out tonight?
Our paths aligned, please don't equivocate
For some strange reason, I wanna know what you were doing out tonight
But you never even saw my face
And you just left like nothing happened, turning off into the night

Now I'm left to think again
I can't get you out my mind
My eyes so focused and I almost met my end
You turned left and I turned right
I got first and you got second, but still we're both in 10th

I feel the pull of the night sky
The earth feels rounder than before
I think it's strange, but the stars don't look quite right
And now you're gone, I don't know what's real anymore

We'll never meet again
But I don't think you even met me in the first place
So let me introduce myself
In case you meet me someday

You've got that look in your face
You're not ignoring me to act all tough
In your mind, there's nobody but you out here tonight
You're not trying to take our crap because you've got yourself and stuff

Enjoy your ride
I hope it never ends

You're a mystery
Girl, you're a mystery
This life's a mystery
Girl, I'll solve this mystery

Enjoy your ride
I hope it never ends

Hope You Die

She said, "Nothing last forever
Everything, even our love
Must come to an end
One day our love will die
And we will go our separate ways"

But I said, "No," and then I told her
"If we try, even our love
Can make it to the end
Until one of *us* dies
And only one is here to stay

That got me thinking
Life without you would lose its meaning
Each day that goes would bring another tear
I don't want you to have a thing to fear

So I hope you die before I do
I love you more than life, I do
I don't want the weight of losing to be placed on you
I don't want to die, not knowing how you'll do

I'm trying to be selfless
Or am I being selfish?
For wanting to live a longer life than her

But that's not my point here
I'd go crazy without her

I'll live all alone while she rests in peace

I'll take the long road
You take the high road
I hope you had a good life down here

With me
You'll see
You have nothing to fear

I hope you die before I do
I love you more than life, I do
I don't want the weight of living to be placed on you
But I guess fate will have to choose

So just take us at the same time
Just take us at the same time
Please, just take us at the same time
Just take us at the same time
But if we can't have that

I hope you die before I do
I love you more than life, I do
I can't imagine a life in a world without you
But I'd take it any day, to spare it from you

Ren's Law

I'm caught under Ren's Law again
Trapped in four walls of solid brick
Vessel to its dock, nothing's gonna stop
It from making it's landing
Standing in the valley
Don't know how I got here
But the water tower in the distance
Gives a reminder of my resistance
And my pathetic persistence
Slowly sinking in my own spit
I know I should already know this
Yet I stay stuck on my own stance
I'm just tryna be honest
But it becomes a contest of difference

The walls charge their fees
I'm hungry, you'll only last 10 more minutes
I'm so confused
But this seat offers me it's protection

I can't go there, I won't go there
But I won't go anywhere without you
You can't go anywhere without me
But what do I do?
I never want to go without her
But she could go without me
Stretched apart from this one city

Bridge the river
Of his deliver–
–y two times the time
I'm not doing fine
Alright, fine
This time I'll defy my mind
When I hit the stop sign
Walking down the street through the lines
I've already signed
With curls, dots, and lines
To give promise of mine
The eyelines will highlight
How your eyesight will find mine
Then I realize that it's got a co-sign
From those who don't know mine
My hand's got a quiver
I wish I could go quicker
But you give me the finger
Oh, our lonely laughter lines linger

I'm down on my knees
Begging for your attention
My heart is bruised
And I've lost my direction

I can't go there, I won't go there
But I won't go anywhere without you
But she could go without me
Stretched apart from this one city

Noah, Please

You're my sun in this empty sky
You're the clouds when there's too much light
You're the rain when my skin's gone dry
You're my moon in a starless night

You're my shield in a losing fight
You're my sword when I'm out of flight
You're the reason that I still try
When I feel like I just could die

You're my cheek when I need to cry
Let my tears roll down your smooth side
I'll make an ocean that we'll have to ride
'Til the dove comes to say we've survived

Have I done enough?
For you to take me with you
I'll give you all I have
I'll give you all I have
Am I bad enough?
For you to leave me behind
Swallowed up by the ocean
Under the arc of the chosen

If I lose by my own mistakes, is it suicide?
I'm scared soon we'll be apart, no more you and I
When the flood comes, will I get a ride?
And if not, then just know I tried?

Noah, please
I'll make it worth it
Just don't leave me
When the oceans flood in

Noah, please
Tell me if I'm doing good enough
And if not, I promise I'll do better

Lost (Prologue)

Lost,
Never a more relatable word
I'm lost, feeling more than unsure
About my future, about my place in this world
Lost in the echoes, feeling so insecure
Like a feather that lost its bird
Like an "I love you" that's not returned
Like a seed that can't find the dirt
Like a calf that can't find its herd
Like an old man whose vision's gone blurred
Like a song you wrote that's never been heard
Like a mother when her son hides away from her
Like every one of us is in regard to our future
And so on, I could go on forever
I've always known that this would hurt
But not like this, not like this

My life's gone to pieces
And I need to arrange them
Before I can return

[

...

]

Found (Epilogue)

[

…

]

I want to be,
Like the song you forgot but know you once heard
That you find one day with a quick Google search
Like a bird that flew all the way over the ocean and finally found its perch
That moment when your long-worked idea finally works
All life's lessons lived and learned
All the achievements in your favorite game finally earned
Like Cinderella and the prince when the glass slipped worked
Finally getting the love they deserved
Like the feeling of home when you finally return
I always thought that I would learn
But I still search, I still search
Lost and afraid, it's more than I can take
I can't take this, can't take this
I still chase it, still chase it
Hoping that one day, just one day
I'll be found, I'll feel proud

600 Ft. Above the Ground

How can uncertainty bring you to a place of humility?

I'm falling again
600 feet above the ground you're standing on
I feel the wind
It tries to hold me up
But I know it won't be until I hit the ground that I will finally stop
Finally stop falling
I've given up
No parachute to guide me safely to the ground

Humility

I'm falling again
But I am lifted up
By the feeling that no matter what
No matter if I die or not
I still have some time left to live
So I'll try to make the best of it
Though the uncertainty of certain death
Tries to steal away my breath
Sometimes I feel there's no hope left
But that's not true, I'm not dead yet
And I can make this better if I try
Even as I'm falling through the sky

Just don't let the time pass you by

"he needs the humility to accept that their way may be better"
(^ example from Google definition of 'humility')

Movie Trailer

I know you like to have your future spoiled
The rest of your life in the palm of your hand
You try to get me to sit down and watch with you
But I won't and I don't think that you understand
I don't want a taste of my best moments
I'll wait and I'll savor them when they arrive
I don't want another preview for my life
I'll sit back and I'll watch this show in it's own time

Brown Eyes (When We Were Beginners)

There's a shooting on the corner of 8th
Please, don't tell me after another 3 that this'll be our fate
I don't want a fight from disagreement
I want to see you through clean eyes
I just wish that you could see it
So I could sleep weightless tonight

So much light is absorbed, but so little is reflected
I hope I'm still more than the me I've projected
Where did the time go? It's already five
I feel like I'm dying but never felt more alive

Will you see me when nails are buried in my brown eyes?
Will you see me when the forest creeps in around me growing thicker?
Will you see me when I don't see you?
Will you still see me, like when we were beginners?

I took a right when I should have gone left
Now these thoughts in my head are all I have left
When you stepped in, I knew I should have had them sneak out through
the back door
But I knew I couldn't hide it anymore
Are you sure you want to see me anymore?

'Cause I can't bear it when the trees fall
But there's no one there to hear the sound
But I don't want this to be our downfall
I want to keep you around

Will you see me when the clouds surround my jawline?
Will you see me when the fire swells up around my beautiful figure?
Will you see me when I don't see you?
Will you still see me, like when we were beginners?

Take me back to the beginning
Please, just take me back to the beginning
When connection was so simple
When there wasn't glass in every window
Take me back to the beginning
Please, just take me back to the beginning
Back to a time we were both winning
Don't tell me now you're thinking about quitting

Because we both know: this is only the beginning

Will you see me when my train of thought is not on time?
Will you see me when my mind's consumed by winter?
Will you see me when I don't see you?
Will you still see me, like when we were beginners?

—

I swear I'm not a quitter
My pigeon will deliver
I just wish it could be quicker
But I'm still such a beginner

I'll make you a promise
This is the start of something better
These brown eyes will learn to see you
Until our eyelines come together

I'll be there to meet you halfway in October

Adoration

These hands
Meant to mold your form
Withstand
Broken bones and pages torn
These hands
Can only hold all that you've worn
Wristband
Constricting blood from which we've sworn

All I gave you was my pure and honest adoration
I'm sorry if I may have been a bit impatient
But right now there's nothing we can do to change it
You provided the canvas and I painted
I'm sorry if you didn't appreciate it

Hey

"Hey, it was really nice to see you smiling and laughing last night. You looked like you were enjoying yourself. I know you've been struggling a lot lately, but it was nice to see you in a good mood again. I hope you're doing better."

Okay

"I'm really sorry about last night. I saw you went quiet and I could tell you weren't okay. If you ever want to talk about anything, just know I'm always here for you."

—

"I can tell you're really trying and I truly do appreciate it, but I need you to know that if this is going to work, I need you to be in a good place and start to take care of yourself. You have so much potential. I see it; we all see it. But it's up to you whether you are going to reach it or not. I love you and I know you love me too, but I can't have you weighing me down with your issues or growing dependent on me. You need to stand up for yourself. Get the help you need. And I'll be here waiting for you when you're ready."

"Okay"

Tundra

I'm cold
Look up at the cracks in the sky
Why do I live only just to get by?
I'm told
String up the trees, not with red yarn but wire
Muffle your heart and put out all the fire
I'm old
Too old to look back, rethink all that lies under
But too young to lose track of the warmth of the summer
I'm frozen
I'm frozen in here
I must find my calling, but in only a year

Please don't leave me here alone
When—*if* you come back
I'll be gone

Eight-teen

Left all alone
Stripped down naked
All I know now
Tinted, faded
All along I've
Overplayed it
I'm the song my
Heart's the playlist

I hold a red ribbon high above my head
Wrapped so tightly 'round my blood-stained wrist
I try so hard to keep it dry
I'm eighteen, I'm eighteen, I'm not ready to die

All this time
I've been waiting
For something to
Overtake me
Now I'm here and
I can't take it
What I need has
No prescription

I hold a red ribbon high above my head
Trapped in the limits of my tight-held fist
I try so hard to keep it dry
I'm eighteen, I'm eighteen, I'm not ready to die

You try to blind
My left eye
I rinse it out, I still see
Though it burns
I have learned
The strongest fight's not to fight

I left salt
Where it's dry
I feel around, I can't see
As it burns
I'm still sure
The hardest fight's not to fight

I hold a red ribbon high above my head
Wrapped so tightly 'round my blood-stained wrist
I try so hard to keep it dry
I'm eighteen, I'm eighteen, I'm not ready to die

I'm eighteen, I'm eighteen
I'm eighteen, I'm eighteen
I'm just eighteen, already eighteen
I'm eighteen, I'm eighteen
I'm eighteen, I'm eighteen

I'm eighteen, I'm eighteen
All I've seen
I'm eighteen, I'm eighteen
Is what I bleed
I'm just eighteen, already eighteen

I'm eighteen, I'm eighteen
Now I see, now I see
I'm eighteen, I'm eighteen
Still I bleed

I'm eighteen, I'm eighteen
I'll learn—I'll learn to believe
But I'm not ready to die

From the Window

I can't go
I wish I could
I probably wouldn't like it if I went
But still, I would
Just so I could be there too
But I won't ruin it for you

I'll just sit here
Staring out the window down at the party across the way
Write a poem or two about some things I'd never say
Play some chords I've never tried before
Wish that I could be there
I hear the music, or just its echo
Either way it doesn't matter
'Cause I'm just watching from the window
I hope you have fun

I'm coming home
I'm coming home
I'm coming home
I'm coming home
I'm coming home
I'm coming home
I'm coming home
I've come and gone

—

I won't fight my feelings
But time has a knack for revealing
My truest feelings in time
I said "I love you" but didn't feel it this time
She's down there and I know it
I can't see her but I know it
And it hurts to know she's right there
But I can't see her though she's right there

And I bet she's having fun
Laughing and dancing
And I'm here in my room
Overlooking from the window
Maybe I could take the plunge
Down to the party
And I could join in too
Would you want me if I did though?

I just want to see you
I want to see you from the window
See your dress through which the wind blows
And all your friends who spend the night's glow
I just want to see *you* glow
I want to see you glow like that, you know
And as I'm looking from the window
There's just one thing that I want to know:

Are you happier when I'm not around?

—

This is not what I thought
How I thought this would go
I just sit here on my phone
And then I'm not alone
I have to go
Though I don't want to
I tell you I'm not busy
Though I had plans for this evening
I was gonna fight with my demons and sorrow
And probably write more sad poems tomorrow
But you all care too much to just leave me here to wallow
I tied a rope around my neck but it's you that makes it hard to swallow

—

On our way out, I look up at the window
This isn't the way today was supposed to go
I still don't have the answer, what would I do if I did though?
Could I have the strength to ever just let you go?

North<>North

She's gone again
I know it's my fault
I can't pull myself up
But she won't be brought down

So why did I come in today?
Why don't I learn to stay away?
I should know by now
If I truly want her to stay
I should learn to give her space
And take my own
When I can't give her the best me

—

I'm alone again
With my phone in my hand
And nothing else

—

I wish there was some way to tell you
How much I want to tell you–
Nevermind, I know I'll just repel you

I'll stay here quiet, I might try to fight it
In these words I'm writing, hide it
You do you, you don't deserve to
Have me around, your whole day ruined

I hope I see you later

—

And then the touch comes in
And I feel like I could cry
It's the way you make me want to live
That makes me feel like I could die

Jealousy (Does He Know?)

Does he laugh
At all your jokes
Just to make you smile
'Cause you know he does that well?

Does he know
How to hold your hand
At just the right times
And to let go when you have had your fill?

Does he hide
All the dissent
Not put up to trial
Or was it even there at all in the first place?

Does he share
All the moments you need
Even ones he won't like
Because he knows how much they'll mean to you?

You never know what's gone until you have it
You never know where to end until you start
You never know what to repair until it crashes
I want you, and you know you still have her heart

But for how long?

—

Does he show you
All your beauty beautifully?
And does he support you
Even when your dreams aren't what he'd like to see?

And does he hold you
So snuggly on that old couch
We used to sleep?
And does it remind you of how we used to be?

Have I already lost you
Without even noticing?
And how come I'm still here
Thinking at 3:37 in the morning?

I know I could still have you
If I would try listening
To you or your family
Or just anyone else but me

You never know what's gone until you have it
You never know where to end until you start
You never know what to repair until it crashes
Oh, can we be happy just the way we are?

And for how long?

—

Does he know when you're sad?
Does he know how to make it all better?
Does he know not to talk about your cousin?
And not to follow in his footsteps now thereafter?
Does he know to give you some time?
You're not one to dive in
Does he know how your hands shake?
And do his do the same?
Does he know where to find your lips?
When your faces eclipse?
Hands just right on your hips?
Does he know how to straighten your spine?
Does he give just the right time?
Before he heads home?
To give you your space after a quick kiss goodnight?

You never know what's gone until you have it
You never know where to end until you start
You never know what to repair until it crashes
I want you, and you know you still have her heart

I want you, and you know you still have her heart
I will do what I have to not to drift apart
Because jealousy has been there from the start

Cold Ton

Driving by to see you on your lunch break
Smiling wide, hoping to put one on your face
Eyes to the side, don't see what's in front of me
My friend almost died; it would have been all because of me

It weighs a cold ton
To know I almost accidentally did it
And it would weigh a cold ton more
If I actually had

Pass it off as a joke as I screech to a halt
I gotta stop being childish, time to be an adult
I didn't even see you, but at that cost, it's not worth it
I almost killed my friend for a wave from my girlfriend

Selfish
Selfish
Helplessly selfish
Selfish
Selfish
Hope-filled and selfish
Selfish
Actions
Taking others' last breaths
Cold and
Endless
One day I'll run out of chances

To the Purple Moon from the Flash Fires

To the purple moon, from the flash fires
I'll be home soon, I've been gone a while
How I miss you, I know you're getting tired
You've got only damp wood, but you still spark the fire

A little fire flashes from the forest
Flowing friskily from the frosty foliage
That he put there like he told he did

And I still want to see you smiling on the surface
Sure it's spreading, sending all these sparks to everything
And this combustion erupts into your brilliance

I got caught in the reverie
I let it get to me
Until it's controlling me

So I'm here to soak in your glow
Knowing I should have listened
To what you're telling me
She casts a light on us all that comes straight from her soul
And just like the moon in the sky, we hear it's alive
But don't listen at all

We've held back the tides as we have grown
But over time I've learned to love your glow
Maybe it's not so bad for love to go
We'll bring a forest fire from the snow

Feelings

Bad feelings
Bad feelings
Bad feelings
Bad feelings
Bad feelings
Bad feelings
Bad feelings
Bad feelings

Oh, you disappeared
No map back to your heart
This is what I feared
I'm losing track of all my feelings

It's my fault
It's my fault
It's my fault
It's my fault
I know

I stayed too long
You got in trouble
I held too tight
Bursted your bubble

I'm sorry if I hurt your feelings

—

You cut me off
And I woke up 12 hours later
But it felt like we went back in time
I can't help but want to ask
Are you losing your feelings?
For me
For me
For me

Or is it just *my* feelings?
Falsifying and denying
Criticizing, uninviting
Oh, she's crying
I'm denying
I'm denying
I'm denying
Say I'm trying
Still denying
I'm denying
I'm denying
I'm denying
I'm denying
I'm denying
Now I'm crying too

^

"Have a good day today,
whatever that means to you"

I hope you're feeling better

Tamagotchi

Hey, sorry for coming around at this time
I just need to vent

Where do I start?
Where do I start?
Where do I start?
Where do I start?
Now it's the end
See? That's my problem
Never know how much I want to live until it's dead and gone
These days respond
With pain and yawns
Try to find the will to take it on
But on and on and on
I get caught in my mistakes
I'm lost at a constant loss
The gun was fully loaded
But I had no strength to take the shot
I'm taking off
To some new place where maybe I can feel on top
I'm feeling off
I once loved life, now that feeling's lost
Left feeling lost
Feel who I've been has only been a fraud
Let's kick this off
Every time I said I loved you
Just know that I meant it, but then you
Said it back and new words came through

Broke the brush, you let me paint you
Poetry in how I see you
Broken pieces lie beneath you
Hopeless, deadly, crying, bleeds through
In the sky, the clouds are see-through
Silver lining, I don't mean to
Come across as if I need you
But if you leave
Then I might not make it through
For too long I've tried to be you
And now it seems that I've lost me too
I depend on you, but you don't need me though
Mi hermosa, tu amigo
I want to live my life contigo
But for that I need to solve my issues
I signed a deal back when I first kissed you
I wish I could see you through the hardships I've been through
And when I'm lost in my head, that's when I most miss you

—

Try to dive for help but it's just kamikaze
Try to hold it back but not a thing can stop me
Crashing over, flooding in, like a tsunami
Press my buttons like a g****** Tamagotchi

Why don't you try and stop me?

—

Struggle turns to feelings to belief
It seems that every time I get too deep is when you leave
I might just have a curse, at worst it's all a tendency
That I'll have with me 'til one day it will become the death of me
Just let me be, I need to breathe and scream while speeding through the streets
My only peace is in these beats and lyrics blasting on repeat
My mind is free, I need to see that someone here can hear my pleas
I'm lonely here with all my fears, so tell me you can hear me, please!
There's so much that I haven't done
And battles that I haven't won
I'm living in a house of one
My sky is blue, without a sun
You have me in your cautious grasp
I can't believe I had the strength to ask
Now a-hundred-eighty days have passed
But I spend every day so scared we'll crash
And instead of trying to make repairs
I drive straight ahead with a vacant stare
Hold your hand to show I care
Disasters always come in pairs
Though I say "I love you," I sometimes feel I resent you
I wish you always made me smile, but I can't just pretend to
And I'm truly sorry if this poem offends you
But I had some things I had to get off my chest too

—

If I needed help, I wouldn't want you calling
Say I hold you back, but you don't try to stop me
Crashing over, flooding in, like a tsunami
Press your buttons like a g****** Tamagotchi

Why don't you try and stop me?

Less Of Myself

I'm not just gonna pretend like I'm more than I am
By making me less of myself

HLHW

She left again
And took the sun with her this time
She took herself right off the map
But for her, the light still shines

I give her everything I can
I give her everything I am
And she says, "Love, you need a plan"
I say, "I love you," again and again

She needs a life without a heartbeat
I need a love without deceit
She needs a life that's always happy
But love, you won't get that from me

And she's so happy
So ha-a-appy
Yeah, she's so happy
So ha-a-appy

—

This love's been a race against time
Trying to prove myself, jumping through hurdles
We've made it around 180
But I promise you I'll come full circle

She needs a life with stability
This is a love that I can't beat
She needs a life that she lives freely
But love, you won't get that from me

And she's so happy
So ha-a-appy
Yeah, she's so happy
So ha-a-appy

—

My love for you is still so strong
To me you'll be here 'til I die
The only question left is
Will you be there by my side?

And we'll be happy
So ha-a-appy
Yeah, we'll be happy
So ha-a-appy

—

I love you
Soooo much
And I just want to make you happy
You know what they say:
"Happy wife, happy life"
You know what May Parker said to Spiderman?:

"A man needs to put his wife before himself"
But I think it's all backwards
It should be:
"Happy life, happy wife"
And:
"A man needs to put himself before his wife"
And I mean no disrespect
But a man must make sure he's taking care of himself
Before he can take care of someone else
For her sake
Because I can't give her a happy life
Unless I have a happy life to give
And I can't give anything to my wife—or anyone
If I don't have a will to live

I have so much fear, I put myself in a cage
And I drag you in with me
And even though I try to fight every chance of escape
I truly don't want to be stuck in here
Even though I say this is the person I am and always want to be
It's honestly not

I hold myself back so much
And I know, in turn, that holds you back too
But I'm letting you know that I got up this morning
And I spent time thinking about all of this
I focused on what's really important to me now
And I made a plan, I wrote a list, I set some goals
I won't tell you what it is right now
Because I think it'll all mean more this way

And you'll understand over time
I just want you to trust me right now
Please, just don't give up on me quite yet
And if I fail, then we can think about ending this

I'm not who I want to be right now
And I think with you I can find good balance
And I think I can give you life

I'll call a therapist tonight
I'll get my first appointment set up
I'll take better care of myself
And I'll give you more time to be you

And I promise, this is something I can do
And I'll do all both for me and also you

—

I know I haven't quite kept all my promises in the past
But I'm telling you that this is my last chance
I'm making that decision
If I can't make this work with you this time
If I can't find the will to let you have the happiness and success that you
deserve
If I can't get into a better, healthier state of mind, and learn to live as an
adult
If I can't love you enough to make things better
Then I'll let you let me go, no matter how much it may hurt

Because I want you to be happy
Even if it's not with me
But right now I'll try my best to make both of us happy
So you can live a life with me

Because,
You make me happy
So ha-a-appy

Make Or Break ƐƐƐ Tracks

I wish I was a bird
So I could fly across the sea
I wish I didn't hurt
So you could fly along with me

It's our time to make or break
We've come a long way from our lake
I'm trying to break my habits for your sake
Before your weary heart will break

She snaps the twig, right on track
Off the rail, but I've got your back
There's so much left that I still lack
I've lost my hope but I want it back

You grabbed my hand
And I held yours too
But I don't understand
Why you let go so soon

It's our time to make or break
We've come a long way from our lake
And if you ever choose to walk away
I know my weary heart will break

I'm running out of chances
We took our chances
And it's a chance I'm glad we took
But this is my chance to show you
How much I want to let this work

Because I know it can if I let it
But I keep holding us back
And if I keep following your rails of change
I won't regret it
But my train of thought keeps leading me off track

It's time to finally set myself on track
It's time to bring us back

Ruin Your Life

This is one of those times that I have doubt in when you say that I don't bother you or stress you out. I feel like I'm ruining your life right now. Actually, I couldn't do that because you're independent or whatever. You don't need me. You could easily just pass me by and leave me behind. And that worries me a lot.

Milk

You were born a rose
But turned to stone
And all you have to tell
Are the secrets you won't
This isn't all you know
I know there's more below
But you've grown such cold bones
That you can't hold your own

—

These falling purple lilacs
Bring back thoughts that bring me right back
To when your life was alright, on the right track
And all that she has is all that you lack
All you want is all that, but she stabs in your back

A perfect incision, when she made the decision
To break, to partition
No blood on the benches, no hurtful intentions
Just me and you sitting, a foot or six distance
Six months have been ended, by our opposition
Our love was magnetic, so close it caused friction
That was not my intention
A black cat passes by, don't believe superstition
Oh, what am I missing? Oh, what am I missing?

Conspiracy theories are all that I'm hearing
And all I've debated is secretly searing
All the time that I've wasted to leave you left leaving
Over time I've still hated myself for not being
The person you dated who'd stay 'til the ending
But I am still going
To try and reform me
From all that you've known me,
Though I know you'll still know me
For who I was always;
I just want you to notice
All of your influence
'Cause all I can do is
Somehow try to prove this
To you; is it true if
I do this for me, not for you
You would hit the undo,
When I'm on the same page as you?
We'll try to rewrite our story as two

I would do anything for you

—

I spilled it all on you
Never got quite enough from you
Now I won't get anymore from you
But there's no use is crying
Have I really been trying?

I was born a rose
But turned to stone
And all I have to tell
Are the secrets I won't
This isn't all I know
Do they know there's more below?
But I've grown such cold bones
That I can't hold my own
I think of all the life you have shown
To me all was unknown
All my life, I've put together a play, thanks for coming to my show
But I guess you have to die in order to grow

Jealousy (You Should Know)

[Quotes from "Star Trek: Voyager" Faces; said by B'Elanna Torres and Tom Paris]

"So strange
When I was a child
I did everything I could to hide my forehead
I grew up in a colony on Kessik IV
My mother and I were the only Klingons there
Nobody ever said anything but
We were different
And I didn't like that feeling
Then my father left
When I was 5 years old
One day he was there and the next he wasn't
I cried myself to sleep every night
For months
Of course I never told anybody
And then I finally decided that he left because I looked like a Klingon
And so I tried to look human"

"Looks like you finally got what you wanted"

—

Who would know
After all this time
Of us intertwined
Such a perfect thing would come to such an end

I didn't know
How to love me first
Not what you deserved
But I guess we can continue on as friends

So we'll go
Our separate ways
I still see your face
But not like I could just the other night

You should know
I still love you loads
But my heart, it knows
It's a chance to take control back of my life

You never know what's gone until you have it
I should have taken care of this way back in March
You never know what to repair until it crashes
Nine words I wish I knew straight from the start
Oh, it's my fault

And I know
It was wrong of me
To assume that we
Could mend this torn up hoodie so quickly

I should go
Should leave here now
Before we drown
In the dryness of everything we're missing

How'd I not know
That this would come?
I pushed my luck
I couldn't help but feel you were my truth

I know it's gone
And I won't fight
'Cause it's my time
To show myself the love that I showed you

You never know what's gone until you have it
I wish I could take this story back to March
You should know how to repair before it crashes
Nine words I should have followed from the start
I know it's my fault

I know I made her sad
And I can't make it better
I know I held her back
Saying sorry won't matter
We have such different dreams
That we can't sleep together
In the opening scene
Way back when I first met her
I was so scared to start
'Cause then I'd love no other
And if we were to part
I knew I can't recover
I thought surely we would be

Together forever
But can we please just still be
Like best friends forever?
Who knows?

Promises I made have long-since been overdue
Excuses I made have worn out, been overused
Got me a therapist to help me get over you
I tried my best, but what was I supposed to do?
Looking back through all the poems I wrote for you
Seeing dozens of poems I never would share with you
Filled with all these dark things that I wrote down because of you
Hey, but don't get me wrong because I really still love you

You should know...
You should know...
You should know...
I didn't know

You never know what's gone until you have it
I should have taken care of this way back in March
You never know what to repair until it crashes
Nine words I wish I knew straight from the start

I will prove to you that I improved a lot
Show you all the happiness you'd ever want
So that jealousy will be there on your part

—

"Okay so. I know this must hurt so much. But I promise it's gonna be okay again. I've been so low after a breakup. And now I'm so happy again. I promise you it'll be okay again. Take care of yourself. Drink water. Dance. Do what you like. What if you put all the love you put into her, into yourself. How beautiful would that be"

[Quote by B'Elanna K on YouTube]

Looking Out On The Lake . . .

Looking out on the lake of our future
Still standing on the cliffside, I wish we'd reach the beach sooner
If I want to be brave, it's my time to prove it to her
To her I'm still weak, but I will be strong in the future

There's so much to live for
And people to die for
But still I don't know
What I live my life for

If you were a wave
I would let you crash over me
If you were the sea
I would drown in you any day

I've been trapped in the reverie
And still don't know what's best for me
Maybe this wasn't meant to be
Maybe you weren't meant for me

We stand on a cliffside
Looking out on the lake
We could jump if we wanted
But we're scared hearts will break

Looking out on the lake of our future
Our love is a lake and the waves will get smoother
Still some hesitation as I ask you, "Are you sure?"
You smile and say, "Our love is a lake and this lake is our future"

. . . .

We missed our chance
This lake's gone dry
The final dance
Our quiet eyes
If you love her
Let her go
If you love her
Let her know

We missed our chance
And now we cry
Maybe this lake
I will fill in time
For me to love her
Let her know
To ride the water
Let it flow

The Most Beautiful Smile

The two of us
Walking different paths
You can't even trust
What's up with that?

I board the bus
You drag behind
Then make a fuss
How it's a waste of time

Hey, come on now
Don't be a fool
You've only got a few months left to prove
That you want to be by my side
Even though that means sometimes I'll ride
A way that you maybe won't
But I won't ride alone

I don't want to say goodbye
I don't want to leave you behind
You've got the most beautiful smile
But I can let that go
Because our time has shown
That you want to make things right
But, boy, I'm not gonna live my life held up tight

Not even your smile could pull me back anymore

Hey, don't get it wrong
Please know I still love you
I'll always be here
But you need some bone to come through

You wrote me a song
And I know it was true
But I think that we're over
It's time that I choose

The Loneliest House

Oh, she starts yelling
And you pick it up
Throw back the curtain
And let it all out

You just want to get out
And she holds you down
Is this the loneliest house
Throughout this whole town?

You plead that you're trying
And she says you're not
"F*** you, b****! D*** it!
I'm not the one who's at fault!"

The screams getting louder
And I'm sitting alone
How do we see each other?
Is this house even home?
But I'm still stuck to this mattress
Looking into my phone
Searching for some sort of comfort
In a comforting tone

You checked in last Wednesday
Because she said you should
Monday comes around
Again, you promised you would

But she doesn't see all your effort
Only sees on the surface
And you both don't understand
How much you're making me nervous

How I want to hear some laughter
But this war still goes on
What if we see each other
Through the pros and the cons?
But she's become an actress
In your eyes, she's a clone
Because we're all actors
Through and through to the bone

I'm alone
I'm alone
I'm alone
I'm alone
I'm alone, I'm alone
I'm alone, I'm alone
I'm alone, I'm alone
I'm alone, I'm alone
I'm alone! I'm alone! I'm alone, I'm alone
I'm alone! I'm alone! I'm alone, I'm alone
I'M ALONE! I'M ALONE! I'M ALONE! I'M ALONE!
I'M ALONE!!! I'M ALONE!!! I'm alone

—

You make it up after
With a call on the phone
Over time you'll recover
But not on your own
We've been driven to madness
Stuck together at home
Will things ever get better
In this hostile zone?

The screams getting louder
And I'm sitting alone
How do we see each other?
Is this house even home?
But I'm still stuck to this mattress
Looking into my phone
Searching for some sort of comfort
In a comforting tone

The screams turn to laughter
I'm no longer alone
We can all see each other
This house is way more than home
But really I'm still here on this mattress
Passed out next to my phone
Searching for some sort of comfort
In my dreams all alone

Is this the loneliest house?

Streets, pt. 1) Rows of Chairs (Streets, pt. 2

I went out on the streets today
Just so maybe I would see your face
But you don't even look my way
As you drive by and to that I say

What does it matter?
I've already lost it all
Oh, what's the matter?
Don't you even care at all?
I guess not, I guess not
I guess not, I guess not
I put in so much effort
But you won't even know
All I want, all I want
All I want, all I want
A little understanding is all I'm after
But I guess there's no hope for me in this cruel world
I guess not, I guess not
I guess not, I guess not
So I'll head to the streets
Now all flooded with seas
But it's all there for me
Because my world is ending

)

When you look out
On the rows of seats
I'll be there in the crowd
With your family
But I have my doubts
That you would want me
So I might not be there
In the rows of seats

I imagine you there
Sitting there in your seat
Playing your violin
So beautifully
All I want is to see
You playing your strings
But I keep questioning
Would you really want me?

No, you don't want me
You think I'm diseased
But be honest, please
I know I'm not there mentally
But anyone can see
How hard I'm trying
And how much it all means to me
So would you please
just let me be
in the rows of seats

(

After the show
I plan to exit stage right
Come to me, death
In the dead of the night
You never should have
Let me out of your sight
I have no defense
You were my shield and my knife

No more fear, I enter the storm
Like nothing could ever stop me
I have suffered enough, so I'm ready to go
Free me from all the rain and thundering
Come on boys, let's go play with death
How much do you really want me?
Or am I not worth enough, so you'll just let me go?
Forever stuck with my pain and suffering

Why don't you love me!?
Tell me, why don't you love me!!??

I went out on the streets today
Just so maybe I would see your face
But you wouldn't even look my way
I know you wouldn't even look my way

Her Neptune

There's a vision of the past I know
But I can only see it through a kaleidoscope
My memories and feelings lost every day that goes
In the fragmented spiral hiding tidal waves of pain I hold
I try to hold onto the wind even when it dies down, like the hawks still fly
on
I've carried salt since I was eight, and it just gets more heavy as more piles
on
Oh, I play in the cold, scold old, bold, and told
The whole world to fold over all they call gold
If it's not what I sold
I've been standing on islands losing fires and family
Ignoring all the questions my heart has been asking me
My hands were destined to lose you, but I'm still falling slowly
Now there's a special silence in the night we met, hold me
Just give me the future, distort the way you see me
And we'll be levitating 'til we break through the ceiling
I've just been drifting, drifting, drifting
And I'm tired of monotony
I want myself to let me go
And I know that's all you want for me
Too
I never got my final show
Because I never saw it coming
But you knew it the whole time
And I lost the rhythm but I'm still humming

Honestly, I've been helplessly searching through the raging sea
For some sort of honesty, but all I found were some ocean dreams
It's time to give me your shoulders and let the flood out of me
The light was upon us but still too far out to reach

You showed me kindness but it wasn't an act
Now my back's against a wall of all that I've lacked
I still hate myself but I keep my head above ground
You cut through me in the best of ways; *I am silence, you're the sound*

Stay close to what's true as the sky goes dim
Fearing the thoughts of you thinking of him
Your love came like summer clouds, now I'm scared of the sun
I'm sentimental if nothing else, hold tight until you're gone

If your quiet eyes are still awake, you love to keep her safe
But I've been told that it takes two to break
I've been scared to fall in love, but if it's real then I'll stay
And if you stay then I'll redecorate

If we ever part, then to each his own
I'll sit back and watch the beaches burn
But I don't want to see the way you see me
When you're seeing somebody else who isn't me

When you lose your flow, vent to the forest fires
I tried to let go, but couldn't break my wires
Why did you love me, a broken child?
Why did you call me? You shouldn't have dialed

Someday you must leave everything all at once
You take me apart in the dark like the birth of a sun
I've been driving for hours, now years wash over me
The moonstone pulls the stars into land meant to be
Your ghost is a lighthouse forever guiding me
To the person that, someday, I want to be
Over time you will tame your sea, rule the waves
The light of Neptune will keep you safe

Porch

All the ghosts are out tonight
And I'm still hiding from the faces
Of all the ones that I have loved
'Cause over time my mind replaces
The pristine figure who you once were
With a reflection through a mirror cracked and jaded
And now I finally see you once again
And realize you're one I never should have hated

Fast forward to a year from now
Let's say that I am past it
That those ghosts all turned to ashes
And I'm the one who lit the matches
Shouldn't I then feel so proud
Instead I sit there sifting sadness
I feel so useless when I think about this
But maybe I'll find gold within this madness

Everyone else has a costume to wear
While I sit on the porch in my skin and my hair
And no one approaches 'cause I'm already scared
And I'd love to come find you but tonight I'll fight fair

If there ever comes a day
That you'd agree to be again
I'd put all the past away
To make you happy 'til the end

But if that day never comes
I've written notes all up the streets
And though I'm still hoping that it does
At least you won't forget your place in me

Everyone puts on a costume of care
And shows me all kinds of kindness I know is not there
I wish I was a ghost so I could vanish in air
But I still haven't seen you, but after last week, I'm scared

But still, I just can't help but want you to find me
Though I know I don't have anything left to say
So I just string all my feelings along in this writing
And though I'm feeling dead, I hope you're doing great
And I'll stay out here just waiting and waiting and waiting
'Cause I can't go inside, I wanna give you your space
But sometimes being lonely can be more than frightening
So in my head I make scenarios where things all go my way

I'll come 'round the porch and there you will be
With no mask on your face, just that green and white tee
And you'll tell me you love me and how much I was missed
And it'll all feel so perfect like the first time we kissed

Time passes and passes as midnight draws near
And I'm still all alone sitting without you here
People come and they go, they will all disappear
But to lose myself now is my biggest of fears

I come 'round the porch and you're there waiting for me
I run into your arms and we sit there on the swing
Your hand in my hand and your heart in my chest
Rising up to the ceiling like the smoke of the past

We all love to dream but we know love never lasts

Seconds (Interlude)

"I'm sorry about you and [her]. I'm sorry you are feeling lost. Sadly, the person one might fall in love with at 16 years old doesn't always end up the one they find themselves waking up next to when they're 30 years old. There is a lot of growth and change in the teen years. I do hope that you atleast realize that both you and [her] are better people for having loved one another. You've experienced 'firsts' together and helped each other grow in ways you hadn't before you were in one another's lives. Because of you, [she] knows what it's like to truly love a person that's not in her family. I don't know where your paths will end up in the future, but I do hope you will always plan to be around, talking about music with me, showing me your drawings/paintings, eating our fancy food and sharing stories with me about your life. You are an incredible human being, Jaedon. I'm glad my family has been given the opportunity to know you. I'll always be here to listen, if you need an ear. Keep your face to the sun and keep moving your feet forward. You're going to be okay."

[world in my hands]

I've got the world in my hands
But don't have the means to hold it
The right cards are up next
But I already folded

You're a flower in my garden
Through this season of drought
I don't blame you for worrying
You have reason to doubt

whatyouwant | deenitahw

White roses line your arms
But time has brought them disarray
The cinders of beginners left
A shell of modern age
Your melody is telling me
We'll sprout through the cracks one day
I've learned my lessons about what happens
When you let stress get in your way
And you can't stress enough to me
That this can't happen without harmony
So I can tell you honestly
I won't let the past replay

Staying in my bubble
Has brought me lots of trouble
Ever since I was a kid
And now it's grown
Too big to pop
I don't know if it can be fixed
A blueprint of the future lays
In front of me but in a haze
Written out in only grays
Refusing to show me its face
I know I have the choice to say
That this way is the only way

And that will be the truth one day
But self-assurance lies so far away

What you want mirrors what I need
I want to live so strong and free
You're everything I want to be
Everything I need to be
I've lived all my life so solemnly
But you show my beauty beautifully
And over time you'll find in me
Everything you want to be

Everything you want I need
I want it both for you and me

Circulate my brain
Circulate my brain
Circulate my brain
Circulate the way I'm feeling
Dealing with all of my demons
No repeating
No repeating
Circulate my brain with meaning
Flowing through my wounded being
Tight mesh will be replaced with breathing
My frayed heart was hardly beating
But not since I have been with you
And if I can be there for myself
I'll always be there for you

No repeating, no repeating

My eternal being

Out its cage it's creeping

No repeating, no repeating

Now it's time

Kinetics screaming

Now it's time

The seafloor's bleeding

Now it's time

No more repeating

No repeating, no repeating

No repeating, no repeating...

...no repeating, no repeating...

...no repeating, no repeating...

...no repeating...no repeating...

...no repeating...

...no repeating...

...no repeating...

...no repeating...

...no repeating...

...no repeating...

Baby Dawn

Breaking out into the light
After nearly a year with her
You finally see who she truly is
And then she's gone

Abandoned at the cusp of dawn
The lights dim just a bit
Oh, sweetie, they'll take care of you
Oh, baby, dawn will come

Five days have passed
And she's come back for you
Why wasn't she there to greet you at the gate?
Does she really even care for you?

Pulled right back as dusk sets in
She came back, she didn't quit
Oh, sweetie, she'll take care of you
Oh, baby, dawn will come

But it still stings
It still pulls you to the sea
Back into the water
Like the place you first felt loved
But girl, I'll sing
I will pull you from the sea
You will be my daughter
And I promise you'll be loved

This is home, dear, oh my baby dawn
Our light is always lit
Oh, sweetie, we'll take care of you
Oh, baby, dawn will come

And it still stings
It still pulls you to the sea
Pulling in the water
Like the moon in the sky above
Oh, girl, I'll sing
I will pull you from the sea
You will be my daughter
And I promise you'll be loved

Oh, sweetie, please take care of you
Oh, your baby, dawn, will come
And sweetie, please take care of him
And babe, his dawn will come
Oh, baby dawn, he'll be your sun

Yellow Lights

My words lay in the leftover scraps of a child's play
Holding onto the moments of yesterday
Hidden inside these lines I know some may hate
But can you please forgive me 'cause it's all homemade
Thinking back on these times staying up too late
Sinking inside these rhymes 'til I suffocate
Wasting all of my time thinking I'm still eight
I need to catch up, just hope that it's not too late

Spinning all up in my head, upset, demons oscillate
Beaten by my own words like a lost debate
I can't follow all the rules that you obligate
'Cause every time I've tried I have almost lost my way
After 18 years I've got a lot that I gotta say
Dropped out of college after 2 weeks, I couldn't stay
I know I made you sad, I know that you're not okay
I promise you all someday I will find my way

I'll sit here on your front porch until you feel better
'Cause who am I when we're not together?
I need to find a way to get you out of your head
But I still can't find a way to get out of my bed

The beast in me is running free
My fears repeating endlessly
I need to be releasing these
A masterpiece in me you see
I don't see what you see in me

On my knees pleading helplessly
For anything to set me free
Can I survive with nobody?

At night I toss and turn like salad and pages
So many wonderful people settle for minimum wages
But I want my work to last all through the ages
But I'm still so scared to take a step, take chances, make changes
If there's one thing in this world that I'll always hate it's
When I tell myself, and feel, that I could never make it
But I am who I am and I put my values over status
And not a thing that exists within this whole wild world could ever change
this

I keep my past around me grasped hella tight
But I keep pushing forward toward mellow sights
There's no one here to tell me what to do or help decide
And as I make my way through this life
I see no red or green, only yellow lights

—

I wish people knew me, I just want to be famous
But if I want to write my story then I've gotta make some changes
Why do we believe that everybody else has got some pages?
I wrote up my own novel, but its contents are sort of faithless
I wanted to be like you and everybody that was next to me
And now I'm all alone stuck at a light like it was meant to be
I wish that I was colorblind so I'm never stuck in jeopardy
And everybody's darks and lights could mix just like a symphony

I thought I had a plan but then I lost it when the summer fell
And took a year off school and spent it learning how to love myself
There's blood left on the intersection, my thoughts start an insurrection
Heard the hurt was an obsession, held my heart up for inspection
Found out all the weight I carried, thought I'd lost but only buried
Deep inside was getting scary; pages tearing, need repairing
Pieces come together and I swear I'm gonna do it
And next time I come to that light I'mma drive straight through it

There is no way I'm holding back
There is no way I'm holding back
There's no way I'm holding back
There is no way—

Kill Myself

Winter's approaching
Fresh starts encroaching
Soon it'll be snowing
All knowing, all knowing

Friends have been ghosting
My family hosting
My burdens I'm boasting
All knowing, all knowing

And I could just kill myself
But honestly what would that help?
At least you won't have to hold me
I'll never do what you told me

My pages are folding
The heat in here's scolding
But it's already snowing
All knowing, all knowing

It's time to get going
But I keep on holding
My mind and yours melding
Okay, I'm going, I'm going

And I could re-skill myself
But honestly what would that help?
At least you can have the cold me

'Cause I'm so hot it kills me

I just want to pull me
Right out of this daydream
And not feel this daily
Not knowing, not knowing

By ticking clock or by resigning
Instill the drop with sacred findings
I need to stop, there's no rewinding
All knowing, all knowing

The snow is all melting
And it hasn't been helping
My skin cracked and welting
I wish I was all-knowing

What if my bones are still golding?
Still, the weight, it's—

So what if I killed myself!?
It's the way that I've always felt
I know how much you now hate me
Everything I've done makes you angry

I can be dead all by myself
Won't ever hurt anyone else
And it could all be so easy
I just hope you never leave me

I know that you knew me well
And you know that I do mean well
So I'd rather just leave you be
I won't forget what you told me

Uranus

You're in us all
You're in us all
Uranus calling
To wash through our walls

You're in us all
You're in us all
Uranus offering
To silence our calls

And we'll be just fine
It'll all be alright

You're in us all
You're in us all
Uranus calling
To sanctify our flaws

You're in us all
You're in us all
Uranus watching
To keep us all from harm

And we'll be just fine
It'll all be alright

You're in us all
You're in us all
Uranus stalling
To go back to your hole

'Cause you're gonna, you're gonna
You're gonna fall
Uranus bawling
To be seen by all

But we promise: you're in us, you're in us
You're in us all
Uranus always
'Cause you made us whole

And we're all with you
Here in Neptune
All of us calling
'Cause all of us want you
Floating above you
The mist overcomes you
Dismissed from our falling
We will come 'cause we love you
And we'll be just fine
It'll all be alright

When You Want Something More

Laying in bed in second grade
Dreaming of who I'd be someday
Thinking nothing could stand in my way
I'll make everyone proud
I've always had a lot to say
Thought I could say them and get paid
Live my life in my own way
But look where I am now

I should've gone to college
And now I'm here held hostage
But I guess that's what the cost is
When you want something more
When you want something more
When you want something more

—

I'm coming back to home to stay
I thought that I could find some space
To create and make myself a name
But there's no one left around
Neglected friends and family
Lost control of my mental state
Now I'm looking back on yesterdays
But I can't go back now

I should have called more often
And now I'm counting up my losses
But I guess that's what the cost is
When you want something more
When you want something more
When you want something more

—

The pictures that you gave to me
The way you paved the way for me
I'd give you all back everything
To give you something more

The issues that I made for you
The days I stayed away from you
I'd take all that you've suffered through
To give you something more

But I can't give you something more
I can't give you *any* more
I guess that's the price you pay
When you want something more

The Littlest Fisherman

Knee-deep here in the sea
Seeking freedom from sleep
But fish and everything bleed
When they get too near to me

One more step and I get her
We gotta keep close together
I'm stacking wood for the winter
To warm her heart, beat my mental

Can't take the heat
Of passion's peak
I overthink
You oversee
Everybody
Who's here with me
Stands up to speak
And they say to me

You're too little to be fishing
Standing there just waiting, wishing
We knew you'd fail from the beginning
Before you fish...

You gotta learn the rules
Learn how the rod is used
You can't go head-first diving in
You'll end up dead-last in the end

Staying steadfast, don't pretend
Is how you'll get it, my young friend

—

Try to mend the dress
Upset the mess
My mind obsesses

I passed all the tests
But failed the rest
My trials endless

Let myself sink down
You won't stick around
High tide recesses

I tried to hide the light
Inside the fright
My find regresses

She slips from me
A catfish dream
Back to the sea
You lapsed in me
And in a dream
You come to me
And so briefly
You say to me

You're too little to be fishing
Standing there just waiting, wishing
I knew you'd fail from the beginning
Before you fish...

You gotta learn the rules
Learn how the rod is used
You can't go head-first diving in
You'll end up dead-last in the end
Staying steadfast don't pretend
Is how you'll get me, my young friend

—

I walked out to the river
See some boys there from the village
Fishing skillfully and honest
Taking chances but still cautious
They invite me in to join them
I tried to stay back and avoid them
But in the hopes of catching something
That could last me, ever-loving
I head over to the shore
Cast my rod out in the waves
All the others reel theirs back
Letting me control the space
And I feel a pull deep in my soul
That's reaching out for something more
And I think of what they said to me before

You're too little to be fishing
Standing there just waiting, wishing
We knew you'd fail from the beginning
Before you fish…

You gotta learn the rules
Learn how the rod is used
You can't go head-first diving in
You'll end up dead-last in the end
Staying steadfast, don't pretend
Is how you'll get it, my young friend

I pull my bait in back to me
I'll learn to fish before I try
Try again to catch something
'Cause I don't want another fish to die

The Birthday Party

I have a month left 'til my birthday
I need some friends there in the worst way
But when they invite *me* I just hurt them
And I no longer want to be a burden

How can I ask them to come
When I'm the one to beat the party down?
How can I ask them to come
When I don't even want myself around?

What would I do if they came?
What would I do if they *stayed*?
I really don't want to waste their time
Better yet, don't be my friend, don't want to waste your life

Without *me*, there is no me and you
But I don't have the strength to see it though
At least I can have my cake and eat it too
But it doesn't taste as good in this empty room

So spare me the sympathy
And the card that cost you $4.63
Go enjoy the day without me
None of you owe me anything

I'll beat myself mentally
I'm in this cycle, it's rinse-repeat
The pain's a taste ingrained into me
It can't be washed out, no Listerine

I should be planning a party, instead I cry on the floor
My heart should be filled with excitement, instead though, my heart is sore
I've got so many issues I try to ignore
I wish I could know someday what I live for

Each candle's a reminder of the years that I've suffered
And the cheers are reminders of the screams that I've muffled
The presents remind me life has nothing to offer me
Who knows how much longer I'll live through this suffering

So when the day comes, I'm sure to be home
And it'll probably be one of the worst that I've known
I know I'm worth nothing, I've cut myself to the bone
I know I'm worth nothing, so I'll spend my birthday alone

Deep Eyes_

My deep eyes
They show me a world
I know that it's real
But I feel that it's not

My deep eyes
They bring me a scene
It all seems so real
But what does it mean?

Standing on the edge of death and reality
How did it get to me?
Is it all meant to be?
I have had Enough of death and reality
Where is the rest of me?
Fading from memory

My deep eyes
They show me a world
I hope that it's real
But I fear that it's not

I realize
It's not what I thought . . . *it was brought for a reason*
Is it all that I fear?
Or is it all that I want?

Standing on the edge of death and reality
How did it get to me?
Is it all meant to be?
I have had Enough of death and reality
Where is the rest of me?
Fading from memory

Fading from memory
Fading from memory
Fading from memory
Fading from memory
Fading from memory
Fading from memory
Fading from memory
Fading from memory

This ground has been strung to me
The comfort lies underneath
A beast coming after me
And I might just have to flee
This time won't be long-lasting
Living only as half of me
But I saw it so lucidly
That it felt just like truth to me
I should be running free
I should be running free
These feet are the enemy
They'll be the death of me
Oh, where is the rest of me?
Falling so endlessly

Fading from everything
Hung up uncertainty
What is this meant to be?
The future or memory?
Warning or comforting?
Demonically or angelically?
Death and reality
How did it get to me?
Was it all meant to be?
Fading from memory
Death is reality
Where is the rest of me?
I've had Enough of me
Fading from memory
Waking from endlessly
Falling obsessively
Reach back for everything
Fading from memory
As if it all gains something
When it's fleeting suddenly
Endlessly suffering
For something that we don't need
And all that I'm left with now
Is the one I could live without
But I'll give it meaning somehow
So that it might just stick around
It's all gone so instantly
It feels like such a mystery
But you'll be right here next to me
Until I fall asleep

Horses_

Melody
The rhythm flows smoothly
It's sad and deep
Makes me want to hug you, tell you everything
It'll all be okay
There's a serene closure to this day
I can understand where your head is
But I wish it was filled with rainbows and happiness
'Cause that's what you deserve
Like horses and the dirt

Yellow
Yellow
Yellow
Showers
Yellow
Flower
Yellow
Yellow
Wear it on your sleeve
Bringing hope and optimism
But I got lost way up in heaven
And I just wanna leave
Nothing left for me
I come from a dark place
Night time in my headspace
I learned in the hardest ways
That love is more that dead weight

Self-hate
Still don't have my debt paid
These hopes and fears I gestate
Twins who fight to get space
Wonder which one will come out in the end
Wonder if it's worth the time that I've bled
I can't take back all the things that I've said
So I guess that I'm probably better of dead
And you say

Melody
The rhythm flows smoothly
It's sad and deep
Makes me want to hug you, tell you everything
It'll all be okay
There's a serene closure to this day
I can understand where your head is
But I wish it was filled with rainbows and happiness
'Cause that's what you deserve
Like horses and the dirt

What I Told You_

You can tell me all you want
But I won't follow what you told me

You keep changing all you want
But I know that you'll never hold me

I've said awful things an awful lot
I've said so many things that hurt you

I just hope that maybe you forgot
I didn't quite mean what I told you

—

I found you in a dream
And I lost you before I woke up

You were a moment
And I couldn't get you quite right

You were too fast and intense
And I got lost in your light

I tried so hard to reach back in
For something that no longer belonged to me

And I lost the purpose
My purpose; I lost *you*

I told you all my darkest secrets
I told you that I loved you

I just hope you forget what I told you
Don't you ever forget what I told you

I'm not modest

I'm not modest
If I'm being honest
I'm just self-conscious
And it often causes
Me to doubt my conscience
And your solemn compliments
I just see my flaws
And all of my losses
So you call me awesome
And I call it nonsense
But honestly it's not modesty
Maybe I'm great to you
Well, but not to me
Why would I play myself down
When I'm already beaten down constantly?
But I do it to myself
I destroy my self-esteem
And nothing seems to help
Feels like I've tried everything
I won't believe a word
No matter what you're telling me
Inside me there's a world
Neglected out of jealousy
I tried to walk away from my heart's cartography
Forge a new path through the forests and along the sea
But I strayed too far from it all and I lost the trees
Nothing to hide me here, no one to talk to me
Miles away from everything

That ever meant a thing to me
But I have a tainted history
Its words are inscribed into me
I tell myself this world still has a lot for me
But reply "I'm just a hopeless wannabe"
This is not the way it ought to be
But the waves still crash and the trees still sway
Letting me know I laid another day to waste
And the pattern replays, copy and paste

I'm not modest
'Cause if I was
I'd have my life more put-together
Right now, it's messier than ever
You say that it's all good; whatever
I know you don't mean it, could you ever
Just tell me the truth? For worse or for better
No matter how hard it is
'Cause living a life full of lies is so hard
And I know it couldn't be as hard as this
The life I want, I've come so far from it
And I'm not here because I wanted this
It's common sense
A broken bird will build a broken nest
So don't offer me your empathy
There's a lot I need to remedy
To cause something to change in me
Then possibly I'll get some peace
Isometry won't mend a thing
Monotony is entropy

Is 'lost' just 'free' in a mess of fear?
You want constancy? Won't get that here
Don't talk to me like I'm great, you see
I won't fall for these fake ecstasies
'Cause honesty is everything
And modesty is dead to me

Leave Before You Go

You can leave if you want
Forget me and move on
Take on the future alone

You can cut the tie
Do whatever you want
But please at least consider
What you'll leave before you go

BLAME

I've heard a lot from you
Look through what I gave you
Pages that I flip through
Beauty turned into mistakes

You've had enough of me
Reaching in subtly
Crawling in under me
Someday you'll see your mistakes

You need to grow up
Don't show up
And act like you know what
You want, there's no shortcut
To get to my heart that I know you want back
No, that won't cut
You tell me to hold up
But don't get your hopes up
Without you there's no us

I won't let you take advantage of me
No more of you micromanaging me
How did it take this long for me to see?
That you're not who I thought that you were
I've had enough of your innocent games
Came down on me with incandescent rage
Now I can see you're the one who's to blame
Might be lost but I know that for sure

—

Now you stand fenced in by youth
Trying to put yourself in my shoes
Writing down all the reasons I'd choose
To move on beyond you tonight

But you fight it, deny it
Remember that time you got violent
I don't want you to be like him
So I'll move on beyond you for life

You need to slow down
And tone down
And act like you're grown now
Go take on your own route
And accept the fact that you are alone now
We're not soulbound
Go home now, it's cold out
It was hard but I know now
Our love could never hold out

Though there are things I won't say to your face
They weigh down on me and I know you won't change
Now I can see you're the one who's to blame
Might be lost but I know that for sure
Might be lost but I know that for sure

Bloody Lip (Northern Lights)

The northern lights
Being torn apart
The choir sings
As you hit the dirt
You just need some time
For your lips to part
You were born to fly
You just need to start

Two vessels have broken
The floodgates have opened
The grime on your face is worth more than you notice
I want you to know this
You're one to be noticed
The light in your eyes shines so bright, runs so deep, it could light the
whole ocean

The northern lights
Being torn apart
The choir sings
As you hit the dirt
You just need some time
For your lips to part
You were born to fly
You just need to start

Come to me when you're hopeless
I will comfort with closeness
'Til you're fine on your own
Life is all that you've known
You're so young, you don't know
Your worth to me alone
Pull the stars into focus
I know you can't control this
A smile from you
Worth a thousand or two
With your eyes, bright and blue
I'll reflect them for you

The northern lights
Have been torn apart
The choir sighs
As you face the dirt
You could reach the sky
If your lips would part
You were born to fly
You just need to start

Seesaw

[Pt. 1: Love is in the Air]
These tiny bubbles fill my blood
Flowing through me, I feel loved
And to you it's just for fun
But to me a whole new life has just begun
Love is in the air
Living life without a care
I want to show how much I care
So I'll write these words to show the world
'Cause I know you're out there somewhere

[Pt. 2: Seesaw]
Walking back inside this morning
She had you on your final warning
You tried to do something kind for a friend
Instead it backfired on you in the end
She yelled at you, said that she'd had enough
Oh, the things we do when we're deeply in love
I start to see all the tears bubble up
Oh, the things we do when we feel we're not loved

[Interlude]
What she sees is not what I saw
I know that you didn't mean any harm
I truly hope you know that she's wrong
What you did is not what she saw

[Pt. 3: Love Comes Back Around]
Heading back outside that afternoon
You tripped and fell, and they all laughed at you
Except for her, her arm held out for you
You took her hand and a chance, got nothing left to lose
I found a note, left there on the ground
It said "Love is in the air", love's lost then it's found
And I guess it's true, love comes back around
I hear my heart beat, a forgotten sound

[Interlude]
What she feels is all of my flaws
I know that you didn't mean any harm
I hope you know I loved you all along
I wish I could go back and see what you saw

[Pt. 4: Kindly-Mend Ours]
Driving home from school that evening
You let out all your truest feelings
Burning through your fuel by speeding
Blasting all your music, screaming
Many people make it through life and get far
Instead we just feel it's time we end ours
Scared to let go of our tightly held scars
Hoping that someday *they'll* kindly mend ours

The Weatherman

Staff in hand
He points it to the sky
Could unleash the greatest storm
Or the prettiest sunshine
Leads them out into the clearing
In the riling light 'til they unwind
Bring out the rain when they get burned
Oh, you're no friend of mine

All is lost at sea
But you control the driving wind
Lightning strikes above
But wave your wand and it will bend
He'd throw the whole sky overboard
And change the weather for a friend
If they were fighting through a storm
But he can't calm the storm within

You cry for time unspent
Your fears freezing down your face
Take them in the forest
Where kites fly above with grace
Call up a snowstorm, call up the wind
Day after day, copy and paste
I've shown you my eyes, my nose, my mouth
But you still don't see my face

Your weathered heart
Pushes and pulls against your will
With a power so smart, so strong, so loving
But with that power, you could kill
I don't know how I served you
And if you're living well
But you left a mark upon my heart
Did you know I think about you still?

Bike Girl

I call her the bike girl
She may look a bit rough but she shines like a bright pearl
So much there up in her head surrounded by those tight curls
She sparks a flame within their brains that in turn ignites hers
And they will huddle close in scarves and coats, just to hear her kind words
She came out of nowhere in the nicest way
Riding her bike under skies of gray
Wore a smile upon a frightless face
She's so young but to them she's the wisest sage
Hey, stay safe on chain links, it's no game to be playing
You all are changing, waging wars on waiting; patience, have it's all that
I'm saying
There's something about that look she's got
Not quite right but not quite wrong
Like she has lessons to be taught
But somehow knew them all along
She speaks with such reverence
They all just wish it could never end
Letting all her words settle in
They once fought, now with her, they are all friends again
She's the star, not the galaxy
She's the brush, not the masterpiece
She's enough, but not everything
Her fears aren't gone, but they're lessening
She has a light that no shadows reach
Singing songs of hope from the balcony
When the road gets bumpy, she keeps pedaling
She stayed a while, but soon had to leave

Bike Girl,
Thank you for your time, you're
Someone I was glad to meet

Hook, Line, & Sinker

[Part 1: Line]
Snow falling, tears crawling
But freeze on my cheek
I'm bawling, it's scalding
My heart flares with heat
It's fine though, there's slight hope
I'm alive still, I guess
Life's a tightrope, no wide roads
I'll grow numb and accept

So do it, I dare you
Hit the nail right on its head
You can bet none of this
Will ever mess up my young head
It's just another thing to talk about with my therapist
A collection of poems I'll write in some time
What!? Do you really think that I'm scared of this!?
Well I'm not, so go ahead and cross that line
I won't stop you

Go ahead and betray me, deceive me
You've got me hook, line, and sinker; believe me
You think I'll follow, no sorrow, naively
I'll just let you both have this home freely
But I won't let you mislead me and cheat me
I can't accept that acceptance is easy
And I'll probably never accept this completely
But I don't hate him or you, I'm just grieving

\

[Part 2: Sinker]
I'll just sink back into my bed
Let the screens invade my head
Until there's nothing left in there
But why should I care?

You cast out your rod, and my life's on the line
But I'm just a sinker, so you know I won't mind
And you're here with this figure
But you're still wrapped 'round his finger
How long will this linger?
How long will this linger?

At one point we were one point
But we were split into two
My life was ruined so there's no point
In me trying to improve
And now our two points turned to three
And you don't care what I think now
Now my life has no point to me
So I'll just let myself sink down

/

[Part 3: Hook]
He's got you hooked and you're all in
To you, none of this is a problem
As long as he can respect her
They can be here together
In the future, the past is forgotten
We've had problems, but maybe he'll solve them
We're so different, but if we have one thing in common
It's that deep in our bones, we know our family has fallen

But while I reach for repair
You hold onto what's there
And accept all the change
Although change is never fair
You could live anywhere
If some family's there
And while I'm left in chains
You soar high in the air

All I wanted was family
In the same home, together
And I would give almost anything
To make our house home, forever
Brother, reel me in
Brother, keep me close
Brother, you're my friend
Brothers, you're my home

LEH

What if
this were
the last song
I ever heard?

A Very Warm Embrace

The third day of that June week
Was the first day of a new life
And I knew right when I saw you
That you'd love me with no costume
Spiraling down in the most beautiful way
I could feel all your light; in your hand, in your face
You took me by surprise, and as I contemplate
You come right up to me with the warmest embrace

So warm
So warm it's almost chilling
So pleasantly warm
Like fresh-from-the-oven cookies at the bakery

You're the baker to my being
Bringing comfort, bringing sweetness
Over time it doesn't mean less
The seemingly endless stretches without your presence
We coalesce and strength progresses
And when you step out through the entrance
Let down all defenses
I think of all I could lose
If the sky came down
Or if just the right gust of wind blew
But from right down in front of me
I hear the most pure...

"I missed you!"

Love is in the Air

Love is in the air
The wind dances with my hair
My skin runs down around my neck
My heart is breathing in my chest

There is love in my heart

Underwater Bridges

My color has been washed away
My etches have been faded
Your stones have all grown worn and mossy
But they still hold the same

Many have walked upon my body
And used it to forge their own paths
In this ever-changing world
We are the underwater bridges

The river digs itself in deeper
As the years run down your face
Coming out your eyes
Take a look back through the window
Reflections mixing with the outside world
The past is what we synthesize

Wide eyes in a tunnel
Refrain from the world they knew
As life's work is co-signed to oblivion
And the passage of time passes through
The waves of the water surround us
Growing deeper, making ridges
Our presence in this world
Merely underwater bridges

We are another daughter's wishes
We are another father's mission
We are the underwater bridges
Looming over our own trenches

While we hold on with desperation
They're the fresh precipitation
Just waiting for an invitation
To build a bridge
It's funny how it never changes

Your world has been forgotten
But still plays its part in modern life
Flowing through the water
Until every mouth runs dry

We are the underwater bridges
We paved the pathways at the bottom of the sea
Our time is short yet also endless
We are the future of the past presently

Fragile Wing

I've seen you grow for so long
And I know you know that you're wrong
When you say that you're worthless and a burden to everyone
Though you may not be perfect, you are worth it to everyone

You're a fragile wing
But you'll fly, you'll fly
Raise your voice and sing
And just try, just try
Sing a song of self-respect
And like the butterfly effect
You'll change all of our trajectories
I'll always remember what you said to me
"This world is everything we let it be
And in this world, you're everything"

You'll never know how much that meant to me

—

This world is everything *you* let it be
And in this world, . . . *you're everything*

we're all broken, and we're just...

You are a masterpiece
And your decisions are the artist
You can be anything
It's your decision to restart it

Even if you don't like where you've come from
You've been broke down and beaten and feel like you're no one
It's never too late to repaint, make a new one
Your canvas is never blank, but white paint is an option

Your past can't be trashed but you can leave it behind
Forge a new path and move forward in time
You may try, and you'll try, and you'll try to rewind
But I'll rewind, and remind you it won't help you find

What you're looking for in life
Take a look at your spirit
It has a lot to say
If you would take time to hear it

I always wonder why I'm here
My mind never gives me a break
I know we all do it to some extent
To get us through, our last defense

These bricks that I'm stacking
Are brittle and cracking
Little by little, I'm lacking

The will to keep stacking
My foundation is weak and
When we feel weak then we tend
To turn hate to a dear friend
And our sorrows are deepened

I've been changed and I'm bleeding
From the pain of believing
I have created the demons
That I carry within me
But some I've carried since breathing
And none of them leaving
Only one way of relieving
No more self-deceiving

So write it down, even if no one else sees it
Reach out your hand, even if no one else feels it
You may be lost, but this art is a beacon
We'll make it through, no matter the season

arranging the pieces (reprise)

And let your heart be open, even if no one receives it
Say what you mean, even if no one believes it
Live your life like you don't need a reason
Because we're all broken, and we're just arranging the pieces

Riding The Lake ^^^ Seagulls

^^

These seagulls see our goals of this sea, so gullible to seeing all we seem to call home, held so close we don't see the goal, and now I'm just a sepal; keep the flowers closed three-fold, but at least I can sleep whole as she goes and I can see it all, from a bird's-eye-view as I fly away from this scene all alone, following behind the seagulls

I was wrong
To think we could make it
To try to just fake it
I brought trees along
The roots held too strong
I wrote you a song
And you didn't sing along
But maybe it's because
The words were all wrong
I was wrong
To think I could change it
To think I could change you...
...to think I could change *me*
I couldn't even face it
Maybe someday, maybe someday
That's what I said all along
It was wrong
These branches still stand
But not sturdy and strong
And I'll never get to ask you
Because I guess you're not the one
We were wrong
I was wrong
Now you're gone
And I guess, I hope you have fun
I hope you find someone
Maybe s—...mhmm...someday
Someday

•

Instagram: @arranging_the_pieces

YouTube channel: Arranging the Pieces
@arrangingthepieces0914

Spotify podcast: Arranging the Pieces by Jaedon Blocker

•

"We're all broken,
and we're just arranging the pieces"

^ • < _

9 7 9 8 2 2 4 5 6 4 0 2 6